CONTENTS

Introduction

INTRODUCTION

Now you are 45, you need a financial plan. You have 15 to 20 years of your working life still ahead, when you will reach your peak earning power. One of your major objectives will be to arrange that afterwards you will enjoy a happy retirement - a further 15 to 20 years after you stop work. How far retirement meets your hopes will depend to a large degree on the decisions you take over the next several years.

The outside financial world has become a harsher and less positive place since the first edition of this book appeared only a few years ago - which makes a plan even more necessary. The world has also grown more complex, so the aim of this latest edition is to guide you through the elements you need in order to form your plan. Make use of all the available ways - talking to friends, newspapers, the internet - to help towards your decision-making.

You may be lucky, when one particular step succeeds so well that it sets you onto the right financial path. More likely, your plan will have to stay flexible in order to gain maximum benefit from changes in the laws and outside conditions. Success will probably come from your making a number of positive, possibly unrelated, steps - taking action to cut your income tax bill while helping to arrange the best bank deal for your son or daughter going to university.

To succeed, you do not have to become an instant expert in areas such as tax or pensions, and you may want to take some of these issues to the professionals. When you seek outside help, you will be that much better placed if you know which questions to ask, and fully understand the answers you get in return.

The chapters that follow also aim to set out the decisions which only you can make - what level of risk can you live with, would you rather borrow than move house in order to raise some cash? This book's aim is to help make your decisions easier and that much more effective.

****

Chapter 1.

HOW TO MAKE A MILLION-GENERALLY

So you and your partner want to retire with £1million in the bank. Great idea - so how do you do it?

Most people would first think of buying premium bonds. They are safe, being backed by the government, they pay out a £1 million prize every month and there is no tax on whatever you win. But the odds against you are huge: around 43 billion to one against your bond hitting the jackpot.

You and your partner can each buy up to £30,000 worth of bonds. These go into a pot, on which the Treasury fixes what amounts to a rate of interest - 0.125% a month or 1.5% a year. This interest is paid out in prizes, ranging from £25 up to the magic £1 million. When you buy a bond, the chances of winning a prize are 24,000 to one. If you do win, the strong chances are that you will get £25.

TWO WAYS TO GO

A wealthy person will buy premium bonds, as one place to invest a small part of his cash resources. At the other end of the financial scale, an average man will buy the £100 minimum, working on the theory that the amount of bank interest is irrelevant - while there is just the chance of a serious win.

Premium bonds have one advantage over a lottery, that you keep your stake. In the UK National Lottery, or any other, when you lose then your capital is gone. When you buy a premium bond, you keep your holding until you cash it in. You just have to reckon on the bank interest which you could have earned - what the experts call the 'opportunity cost' which applies across a whole range of financial decisions.

But you decide that the odds against you are just too great. Over your working life of 40 years there will be nearly 500 monthly drawings of premium bonds which you might think brings the odds of a £1 million win down to 86 million to one. Even on that basis, the chances of a win are just too small. Like most people, the sensible plan is for you to buy the minimum £100 worth of bonds, lock them away and forget them - and one day maybe have a nice surprise.

BE LIKE WARREN BUFFETT

You could make your million by being like a Warren Buffett, the famous US investor - pick a share which will turn a modest stake into £1 million. Apple and Amazon are two recent examples of companies which have transformed shareholders' wealth. Over 10 years Apple turned a £100 investment into £3,900, so that a £25,000 initial stake would have reached your £1 million target. Or think about Priceline, one of the world's leading providers of online travel: over five years, their shares rose twice as fast as Apple.

History and hindsight are wonderful, but you have to find the business that will be the Apple/Amazon of the next 10 years. There are no guidelines here - especially as the company may be operating in China, Russia or Brazil. If you go down this route, think hard about risk and remember the great dotcom boom and bust.

OR GO TRADITIONAL

But all this, you say, is pie in the sky - get lucky in premium bonds, choose the right share. The chances are remote, and there are risks: pick the wrong share, you can lose some or all of your original stake. You decide to go down the traditional route, making regular investments which will get you to £1 million with reasonable certainty and with a low level of risk.

You appreciate that the key is to start early. You decide that you and your partner can put aside £5,000 a year between you. This represents a chunk of your income, but you would have aimed to make some savings and you are prepared to use equity in your home to make up for lean years, if needed.

BUY AN ISA

You put the money into an ISA, where all the growth and the income come free of tax. In 2012-13, you and your partner can each put £11,280 into an ISA (rising to £11520 in 2013/2014) and rather restricted ISAs are now available for your children.

As your ISA income grows, that will help towards the £5,000 a year which you have decided to invest. Your benchmark is a yield of 7% - bond funds can give you rather more, while equity income funds offer rather less. And you know you can always access the ISA in an emergency or if you want to change strategy.

From then on, compound interest takes over - what Einstein called the most powerful force in the universe. If you invest £5,000 a year at 7%, then after 40 years you have your £1 million. You can move the variables: if you and your partner can manage an average £10,000 - especially after the first few years - then you could bring the 40 years down to 30. If you saved your £5,000 a year at 8% rather than 7%, you could cut up to five years off the schedule. For a long-term financial plan, you have brought the risks down, just about as low as possible.

OR CHOOSE A PENSION

There is another traditional route - make pension contributions instead of buying ISAs. Financially, this is more effective than year-on-year investment because pension contributions bring tax relief, whereas you have to buy ISAs out of your post-tax earnings. When you have built up your pension pot, you can take 25% in cash free of any tax questions. You are free to put all of your pre-tax income into a pension, up to £50,000 a year and a lifetime cap which runs into seven figures.

The big difference, going the other way, is accessibility. Once you buy an ISA, you can get your hands on it whenever you want. Once you make a pension contribution, you can only draw the pension when you reach age 55.

There may be legal ways to claw back your pension contributions before then, but you will find them difficult and expensive. When you have bought into a pension, the money is effectively out of your hands until age 55.

TAX-DEDUCTIBILITY COUNTS

So long as you can accept the difference in access, tax-deductibility makes pensions a better financial proposition than a series. If you chose a pension rather than ISAs for your £5,000 or £10,000 a year, and you pay higher rate tax, then the cost comes down to £3,000 or £6,000. Over a long term period, that makes a huge difference.

When you look at ISAs as against pensions, you need to consider how you might use the £1 million which you have so carefully put together. If you plan to use the money for a capital spend - to buy a new house or go round the world - the origin of the £1 million becomes of secondary importance. But if you want the £1 million as a source of income, then the ISA route is more attractive. There is no more tax to pay on dividends and interest from an ISA, but pension income is taxed in the same way as wages and salary - up to 50% then 45% from April 2013.

Taxation probably represents the biggest obstacle to you creating a £1 million asset by making regular investments. If tax becomes an issue, you need to look at the range of tax-efficient investments - including a new, attractive, scheme which started last April.

VCT/EIS?

The two well-established schemes are Venture Capital Trusts, where you invest in a fund, and the Enterprise Investment Scheme, where you buy direct into a business (property and finance are excluded). In a VCT, you get 30% income tax relief based on the amount you invest. You can invest up to £200,000, with a qualifying period of five years. For both VCT and EIS, the tax breaks come only when you buy new shares - not when you buy later in the market.

VCTs invest in businesses where the assets are less than £7 million(rising to £14 million next year)and some managers have established steady records, paying dividends around 7% a year. VCTs tend either to be generalist, or fixed life where the manager winds up the fund after an agreed number of years.

YOU GO DIRECT

Under the Enterprise Investment Scheme, you go direct into a business which is riskier than putting your money into a fund. The EIS, like the VCT, gives you 30% income tax relief on what you put in, but here the maximum is £500,000 and the qualifying period is down to three years.

EIS companies may not be listed - though that means they can be traded on AIM, the Alternative Investment Market.

Since the 2012 budget, the size of EIS companies has been set at £15 million of assets with up to 250 employees.

DEFERRAL UNLIMITED!

There are two other handy features on EIS. You can carry back up to 100% of your investment to the previous year for income tax relief and you can defer Capital Gains Tax - so you can get unlimited CGT deferral through a series of investments. Both VCT and EIS are riskier than traditional stock market investments and are likely to be less liquid - though useful if you are good at picking shares and have an actual or potential tax issue.

NEWEST THE MOST GENEROUS

If tax is an important issue for you, think about the Treasury's latest plan, which started last April. This is the SEIS, Seed Enterprise Investment Scheme, which aims to channel money into company start-ups. The tax break is the most generous yet - you can put in up to £100,000 a year and get tax relief at 50%, regardless of your own marginal tax rate. And it carries the EIS break on Capital Gains Tax.

Just look at the possibilities. Suppose that you make a £20,000 capital gain during the current tax year and put the money into SEIS shares. You save tax on the capital gain, which would have cost you £5,600, and you also get income tax relief of £10,000. The SEIS investment itself will come free of capital gains tax once you have held the shares for three years. (A SEIS fund has been set up, to help finance student start-ups)

If you are clever (or lucky) at picking investments, these tax-efficient investments will get a long way towards your £1 million target - partly through growth in the shares themselves and partly through the tax concessions which put cash in your pocket.

****

Chapter 2

MONEY FROM PENSIONS

Pensions' basic job is to give you an income when you stop working. But they also do two other very useful things - they give you an outstanding return on your money and they are probably the simplest way to cut your income tax bill.

There are two key features of pensions. Any contributions which you make can be offset against tax, up to the level of your salary with a cap at £50,000, and a £1,500,000 limit over your lifetime, reduced to £1.25m from 2013 (with a stiff tax charge if you pay in more). One simple guide to a decent pension - make a salary contribution equal to half your age, so 15% at age 30, 20% at age 40, and so on. When you have built up your policy, and decide to take your pension at age 55 or older, you can cash in 25%, with no tax to pay and no rules as to what you can do with the money. Suppose that you are a 65-year old man, paying higher rate tax at 40%, and about to take your pension. You will have a pension from your employer, and from the State, but you like the idea of also having your own pension pot. This is how it works:

STEP1: Put £20,00 into a pension policy.
STEP2 : Claim £8,000 tax relief - you are a 40% taxpayer - so that the cost of the policy reduces to £12,000.
STEP3 : Cash in 25% of the policy. This gives you £5,000; the policy reduces by the same amount, so you now have a policy for £15,000.

COST CHECK: The new £15,000 policy has cost you £7,000. You paid £20,000 to start with and you got £13,000 back - £8,000 from the taxman and £5,000 from the insurance company.

STEP4 : Buy an annuity from an insurance company. You know that annuity rates have dropped because of the Bank of England's interest rate policy, but you want security. To keep it simple, choose a level annuity (fixed money income) on a single life (yours, so nothing for your partner after you die)

STEP5 : Your best offer is 5.75% which will give you just over £860 a year. Only a couple of years ago, you would have been offered £1,100, but you do the sum: you spent £7,000 and you will get £860.

RESULT : The yield on your money amounts to 12.3% - roughly 25 times higher than bank rate and 120 times better than on your instant access savings account with one of the high street banks. This has to be a brilliant financial move!

You will not do quite so well if you pay standard rate tax, as opposed to higher rate. You will get less tax relief, so the policy will cost you more. But you still do far better than from a deposit with one of the high street banks.

LESS AT 55

You will also do rather less well if you want to take your pension earlier than age 65. The law allows you to take your pension from 55, when your annuity would be worth just over £700. That would still mean you were getting better than 10% on what you spent - a huge figure in today's marketplace. Remember also that this is high-security income, coming from one of the leading insurance companies. No annuity provider has ever gone broke.

You also have to remember that pensions have one big downside - they are inflexible. Once you make a pension contribution, you lose control until age 55 when you can draw on your pension pot. Even then, you cannot get your hands on the capital beyond the 25% which you can cash in. You can only benefit by drawing an income on which you will pay tax.

PENSION OR ISA?

This contrasts sharply with income from an ISA where you have no more tax to pay.(see the previous chapter).

So which is better - a pension or an ISA?

The key does not depend on clever tax calculations. You just need to find out whether your employer puts money into the company pension fund. Assuming that he does, he is offering you a free gift which you have no reason to refuse. Join the fund, put in your share and benefit from what he contributes. From this year, every company with at least one employee will have to enroll them into a pension fund - the timing will depend on the size of the firm.

£50 A WEEK - AS A GIFT

Look at the numbers. Across industry as a whole, employers put in an average 6% of salaries into pension funds. If you are being paid £40,000 a year, you are being offered a free gift worth around £50 a week. So take it - no ISA can be anywhere as good as this. If you are paying in 4% of what you earn(which is typical)the employer's share will push the total contribution to a healthy 10% of your salary. When you come to retire, your pension pot will be more than twice as large as it would have been from just your own contributions. As a financial decision, this has to be a no-brainer.

HMRC HELPS.......

Whatever you pay into a pension, up to the official limits, goes to reduce your tax bill. Given that HMRC are helping, anyone, especially a higher rate taxpayer, needs to think about making pension contributions. The point is simple: if you are a higher rate taxpayer and put £100 into a pension fund, it will cost you £60. If you are a top rate payer, at 45% from 2013-14, it will cost you £55. Making pension contributions is one of the very few ways to cut back your tax bill.

But an ISA buyer will point out that the opposite is also true - if you pay tax at standard rate in a company with no employer contributions, the decision has to be finely balanced. If you have just started in a job, paying 20% tax with no current employer contributions, you could begin by buying ISAs and then move to pension payments as your tax rate goes up and your employer starts to pay in.

MAYBE THINK SIPP

Many people reduce their tax bill by paying into a pension fund, but you can run your own through a SIPP - a Self-invested pension plan. This puts you in direct control of your pension pot, and gives access to a broad range of investments.

You get all the usual tax breaks, notably freedom from income tax and gains tax. But a SIPP will cost, say through a set-up fee and annual charges. You will pay the more flexibility you want in investment choice - so SIPPs are best suited to larger pension pots.

OR STAKEHOLDER?

But there is also a way to benefit, getting help from the taxman, even if you pay no tax at all. With a Stakeholder pension, you get a 20% subsidy and you can start or stop the plan when you want. You can set up a stakeholder for yourself or for anyone you choose, paying up to £3,600 a year.

Suppose you set up a stakeholder plan for your 70-year old widowed mother. She does not pay tax because her income is less than her £10,500 personal allowance. You send the insurance company a cheque for £3,600 less the standard rate of tax at 20%. - so you hand over £2,880.

TAX MONEY TO A NON-TAXPAYER

The taxman then sends the insurance company a cheque for the balance of £720. This is the subsidy, which means that every £100 you put into the pension has cost you only £80. It also means that your mother, who does not pay any tax, benefits from a subsidy given by the taxman. A stakeholder plan is too small to change anyone's financial world. But a subsidy is a subsidy, and you could turn creative - say stakeholder plans to start wealth creation for your nephews and nieces?

MAYBE DRAWDOWN?

Pension rules have been greatly relaxed over the last few years - the big change being that you no longer have to buy an annuity when you reach age 75. Instead, you can keep your pension pot invested and set up a drawdown scheme - to be practical, so long as your pension fund is big enough. If you are looking for security, you will still choose an annuity for life. If you go for drawdown, you will probably need a pot of at least £100,000 after you have taken out the tax-free cash.

Drawdown comes in two types. If you simply leave your pension fund invested, you will be in income drawdown - where you decide how much income you take and when you take it. The maximum you are allowed is roughly the same as you would get from an annuity. The minimum is zero.

YOU CAN BE FLEXIBLE

The second type is flexible drawdown, where you need to show a secure pension income of at least £20,000 a year - say from a company pension while you have built up a private pension which you are putting into draw-down. (You must be able to show a secure pension: income from investments or property will not be accepted) A flexible drawdown lives up to its name - there are no income limits. You just draw as much as you need, when you need it. Drawdown has great appeal: you are in the driving seat. There are negatives, such as cost. With an annuity, you just hand over your money and collect the income. In drawdown, costs will arise from administration and also investment management - unless you manage the fund yourself.

BUT - THE BIG RISK

But the big risk in drawdown is that your fund fails to deliver. A series of bad or unlucky investment decisions will shrink your pension pot and could leave you (absent other income) with a bleak financial situation in retirement. If your pension is going to provide the bulk of your retirement income, you need to think about using an annuity, say to cover at least your essential living costs. Compromise may be the answer for many people about to retire - unless you are quite well-off or a very clever investor. One way is to divide your fund between an annuity and drawdown. You can take this a step further, by mixing and matching over a number of years - a reflection, maybe, of your own gradual retirement programme.

YOUR INCOME FOR LIFE

Like most people, you decide that you are going to depend on an annuity for your retirement income. Doing the deal is simple: now that you are past 55, you take your pension pot, draw out the 25% of tax-free cash and take the rest to an insurance company. In return, they give you an income for life, with a high degree of security. You keep getting this income however long you live and whatever happens to interest rates or the stock market. To get the best annuity for your money you can check on the net or get a broker to find the best deal for you - a good idea if your situation is any way out of the ordinary. An annuity can fit any size of pension pot and there are none of the ongoing costs which arise with drawdown.

ANNUITIES ARE FIXED

The first point to take on board is that once set up, annuities are fixed. You will not be able to change the insurance company or amend the type of annuity. This can be a drawback if your circumstances change - say you re-marry - and it means that you need to get the deal right first time. Many people put their pension fund with an insurance company, and most of them fall straight into a trap when they take out an annuity. They simply sign up with the company they know, rather than look round the marketplace, and lose about 30% of possible income - equal to thousands of pounds over their retirement.

USE THE OPEN MARKET OPTION

When you buy an annuity, you are completely free to choose where you hand over your money. This is the 'open market option' - which may show you that the biggest and best-known companies do not always offer the best deals. You do not have to make up your mind at just one time. It could make good sense to divide your pension pot and buy annuities over a number of years. Your own requirements may change and annuity rates could move in your favour. You will have a cash flow, arising from the 25% tax-free which you can draw each time you buy an annuity.

INCOME FOR YOUR PARTNER

When you agree the terms of your annuity, you have to think who benefits. You face a trade-off: a single life annuity (just you) will pay the highest income, but it will stop when you die. A joint annuity will pay around 10% less, but it means that your partner will still get an income if you die first. You fix the proportion at the start - a 50% joint life annuity gives your partner 50% of your pension after your death. (You can include your spouse, civil partner or a financial dependent)

One alternative to a joint annuity - depending on your personal situation - is to buy a guarantee, which normally runs for five or 10 years and is not usually expensive. With a guarantee, the annuity will still be paid regardless of when you die within the five or 10 years. After all, you could die a few months after setting up an annuity, where a guarantee would ensure that the income went on being paid to your estate or to someone you nominated. You will probably arrange for the annuity to be paid to you monthly. It is possible to have quarterly or even annual payments - but if you choose annual, make sure that you are covered against the chance that you might die just before the yearly payment arrives!

MAYBE OVERLAP

You need to pause and make a choice if you have set up both a guarantee period and a joint annuity - this is known as 'overlap.' If you choose overlap, and you die inside the guarantee period, then your partner's annuity and the guarantee payments would run side by side. Without overlap, your partner's pension would not start until the guarantee was complete.

A few insurance companies will offer value protection for your annuity, which also aims to cover the situation when you die relatively soon after taking out the annuity. A typical value protection deal will provide cover if you die before age 75. If that happens, the insurance company will return the original amount you paid for the annuity less any payments it has already made - though subject to 55% tax. (The Treasury insists on clawing back the tax concessions on pension contributions).

FIXED - OR DOES IT RISE?

Perhaps the most important option to decide is whether you want a fixed or rising income from your annuity. The highest current income comes from a level annuity - where the payment is fixed money terms for the rest of your life. The problem is clear - the annuity is static, so that inflation steadily reduces its buying power and your income is worth less and less over the years. The longer you live, the bigger the problem becomes.

If this worries you, the insurance company will offer an escalator. You could link your monthly annuity payments to an index, such as Retail or Consumer Prices which will give you total protection. As an alternative, you could specify 2% or 3% yearly escalation.

AN ESCALATOR COSTS

The problem is that an escalator is expensive, in the sense that you get a smaller income than from a level annuity. If you chose a 3% escalator, your immediate income would be 30% less than your friend who bought a level annuity - and it would take you 10 years just to catch up.

What to do? If you are worried about inflation and/or are convinced that you will live to a very ripe old age, then choose an escalator. If current income is important, then opt for a level annuity and maybe divert some of the income into ISAs or inflation-protected investments.

HEALTH COUNTS

Whenever anyone deals with a life insurance company, the advice is always: be upfront about any health issues. This also applies when you buy an annuity - but for a different reason. Medical conditions which could affect your life expectancy point to a higher annuity income. One broker estimates that 60% of the over 55s could be eligible, with the average increase in income likely to be 20-25%. More than 1,000 medical conditions qualify, which the insurance companies divide into three sectors - a lifestyle annuity, which could include long-term smoking; an enhanced annuity, which could reflect a cancer diagnosis, and an impaired life annuity which is based on a serious medical problem. To explore this area, it make sense to use a broker and you will need to allow more time for the process.

WHEN TO BUY?

The best time for financial action, the old saying goes, is now. But now is a particularly tricky time at which to be buying an annuity.

One tricky feature comes out of Brussels, with the ruling that insurance companies must offer the same annuity terms to men and women as from December 2012. Rates for both men and women look set to change and it could take the market some time to settle.

WOMEN LIVE LONGER!

Until now, men have received higher annuity rates than women because women live longer. Put the other way, women have received lower annuity rates than men because insurance companies expect that they will have to pay out for longer. The best guess, when this was written, was that men's rates will fall after the EU ruling - the Treasury forecast is by up to 13%, though industry experts look for rather less. The experts think that women's rates may rise but probably show little change overall.

Someone seeking to buy a sizeable annuity would probably be best advised to wait - or at least make an especially wide search of what the market has to offer.

RATES ARE LOW

A more fundamental problem for annuity buyers at present is that annuity rates are low - driven down by the Bank of England's interest rate policy to help revive the economy - which has also increased pension funds' actuarial liabilities. The fall in annuity rates has been sharp, around 20% in only two years, and there seems little prospect short-term that rates will recover.

Probably the best answer to the puzzle is to follow a time-phasing policy. Divide your pension pot into four or five pieces and invest say one piece a year over the next several years. There is the risk that rates might fall even lower, but the odds from now on must be for higher, rather than even lower, interest and annuity rates. Though just when that might happen is another question!

****

Chapter 3

ISA's - GOODBYE TO THE TAXMAN

ISAs, Individual Savings Accounts, play an important part in building up your assets. An ISA is a tax-efficient wrapper into which you can put cash, shares or unit trusts. You will have no more tax to pay on the income you receive nor on the capital gains you realise. You do not even have to tell the taxman about the investments you have made nor what you bought and sold.

For anyone who pays tax at 40% or more, it makes sense to take out the biggest possible ISA every year, using cash or switching existing investments. You move taxable income into tax-free and gradually build up a stream of tax-free dividends, interest and future capital gains..

USE IT OR LOSE IT!

In the financial year 2012-13 you can put £11,280 into an ISA and there is now a Junior ISA for the under 18s where you, or anyone else can invest £3,600. The ISA limits are scheduled to rise each year in line with inflation, but there is no carry-over in either type. Use it or lose it!

You and your partner are allowed to have an ISA each, but not a joint ISA ,so that a couple with two young children could invest almost £30,000 a year in ISAs with no more tax to pay. It is possible, though a little cumbersome, to buy an ISA for another family member - the fund manager will probably want a formal letter of gift.

HALF COULD BE CASH

Rules govern how you can invest your £11,280. Half of that, i.e. £5,640, can go into a cash ISA which amounts to a bank deposit where you do not have to pay any tax. The other half will go into shares or unit trusts, officially called a stocks and shares ISA.

You have two further options. You could put less than half into a cash ISA, with all the rest going into stocks and shares. Alternatively, you could put all your ISA into stocks and shares. If you change your mind later, you can move a cash ISA to a stocks and shares ISA. But you are not allowed to change in the opposite direction.

MONTHLY MAY BE USEFUL

Fund managers are flexible, and will allow you to buy your ISA by paying a lump sum (usually with a minimum of £500 or £1,000) or by installments (generally with a monthly minimum of £50 or £100). Investing by installments can be a useful option, especially when markets are volatile - a they have been since the start of the credit crunch. This is what the professionals call 'pound averaging' where you spread the cost of the investment over a year.

Getting your money out of an ISA, if you need to, is quick and straightforward. The official rules lay down much you put in. not how much you can take out - and there is no limit to the amount you can hold in your ISA's. The limits mean that if you put the maximum £11,280 into an ISA in 2012-13 and then make a withdrawal, you cannot invest any more in the ISA until the following financial year. If you put in £10,000 and made a withdrawal, you could only invest another £1,280 (£11,280-£10,000) until the next April.

CHANGE THE MANAGER

Probably more likely is that some time after you have invested you decide that you want to change your fund manager. Maybe he has not performed too well, maybe you want to switch to investments which he does not offer. To change, you should go to the new fund manager and get him to make the transfer.

Do not, whatever you do, cash in your ISA's and plan to re-invest. Once you have cashed in, you lose the tax-free status and you can only reinvest to the extent that you have some of your annual allowance still unused.

Some fund managers will charge you an exit fee if you move to a rival - as opposed to just cashing in your ISA's. It is best to check, when you first go to a manager, that you are totally free to leave. Some managers may not charge a fee, but will insist on cashing in your investments. Your tax status is safe, as it is not you but the manager who is cashing in, but he will only transfer cash, not shares or unit trusts.

ISA FOR JUNIOR

The big ISA development in recent years is the Junior ISA - essentially, this is a copy of the normal ISA but with the limit set at £3,600. Effective from November 2011, the Junior ISA is open to all the under 18s - unless they were eligible for the last Labour government's Child Trust Fund. That excludes children born between September 2002 and January 2011 - still leaving 6 million who can join, growing by 800,000 a year!

The other rules and the tax breaks are the same - anyone can put in money, with the parents in charge. No withdrawals are allowed until junior reaches age 18, when the ISA becomes their property and turns into a normal ISA. (A useful time for university and after a few years, for the first house deposit).

JUST ONE OF EACH

Because the Junior ISA is smaller, only one cash ISA and one stocks and shares ISA can be held at any one time. Under the original ISA rules, anyone age 16 can take out a cash ISA, so for just two years junior could benefit from a couple of ISA's.

Some people argue that junior does not need an ISA, as all children have their own tax allowance - so that they can have income of £8,105(in the 2012-13 financial year) without paying any tax. But there is one useful area where a Junior ISA could help - if their income comes from assets given by the parents.

If these gifts earn the child more than £100 gross a year (£200 for two parents) the taxman treats the income as if it belonged to the parent - so likely to hit higher rate tax or even 45%. Taking out a Junior ISA, where there is no further tax to pay, avoids this issue.

MAJOR TYPES OF ISA
These are the three major types of ISA:

CASH ISA. Essentially a bank deposit where the interest comes free of tax. Interest rates on cash ISA's compare favourably with those in the taxable market, so the only way to match inflation is to tie up your money for several years. Many people use a cash ISA as their cash buffer - the three or six months' income which careful people set aside for that ever-possible rainy day. And a cash ISA ranks for compensation up to £85,000 - like a bank account - if the company gets into trouble.

STOCKS AND SHARES ISA. You are free to choose from a whole range of investments - any share that is listed on a recognised stock exchange anywhere in the world. Some listed companies offer low-cost ISA's if you want to invest in their shares. You can put commodity shares into an ISA, but not the commodities themselves. Nor can you include fine wine and works of art. You have to follow a special procedure (known in the business as 'bed and ISA') if you already hold shares or units which you want to place in an ISA. You are not allowed to move them direct - you have to sell, maybe taking a hit on capital gains tax, and then buy the shares from the ISA. If you make a loss on the sale, you can carry that forward in the usual way. (Transfers out of SAYE schemes, made within 90 days, escape capital gains tax).

SELF-SELECT ISA. If you know your way round the investment world, and prefer buying shares to unit trusts, you can go to a broker to open an ISA where you pick and mix your own investments. A self-select ISA will cost a little more to set up and run than a typical unit trust ISA, so you need to pay close attention to costs - including a possible inactivity fee. The idea is that the greater freedom of choice, plus your skills or good fortune, will bring improved financial performance.

All the other ISA rules still apply - how much, and what type of investments, you are allowed to buy. You can trade foreign shares, though some brokers may not offer this facility.

ARE ISA's REALLY TAX-FREE?

Purists will tell you that ISA's are not tax-free, since Gordon Brown changed the rules in the early 1990s. To be correct, holding shares or units in an ISA means that there is no further tax to pay. That arises because share dividends are paid after a 10% tax - which now cannot be reclaimed.

For people who pay tax at standard rate, this means that ISA's are of limited value. On dividends, there is no benefit from holding shares or units in an ISA. Inside or outside an ISA, no more tax is due. You still gain by being free from capital gains tax, but remember that you will only face a bill if you make more than £10,600 of gains in a year (the limit set for 2012-13).

BONDS ARE BETTER

Bond unit trusts have been the great ISA success over the last few years - partly because the yields are much better than on cash and partly because ISA managers can get the tax back on bond interest. Outside an ISA, interest on bonds is paid after 20% tax, just like bank interest. Inside an ISA, the manager can reclaim the tax.

Many bond funds also hold shares, so as to give a spread and provide a kicker for capital growth. As a result, the taxman has laid down that managers can reclaim tax so long as 60% of the unit trust assets are held in bonds. All this makes bond unit trusts an especially attractive investment to hold in an ISA.

You do not have to go into a fund to buy bonds. Over recent months, Tesco and Lloyds Bank have issued bonds direct to investors, so you could buy these and put them into an ISA. Just remember that buying one bond issue, even from a household name, is potentially riskier than buying a fund which will hold a dozen or more bond issues.

BUT CASH MAY NOT BE

Putting money into a cash ISA is one thing - holding cash in a stocks and shares ISA gets a little more complicated. The good news is that you can hold, without any fixed time limit, cash which comes from selling investments or from dividends and interest. The bad news is that the manager has to charge you 20% on this interest - which may itself be on the low side - which he sends to HMRC.

You need to note the taxman's wording. He will tell you that this 20% deduction is not income tax and does not have to appear on your tax return. He will leave to you to work out, therefore, that you cannot reclaim this 20% under the ISA rules!

****

Chapter 4

Manage the Holiday Cash

Your holiday in France suddenly costs 25% less - and your neighbour's time-share in Spain has fallen 25% in value. What has been going on? Answer: the euro dropped like a stone, very fast.

The summer holiday will probably be your biggest single spend of the year, so you need to manage your holiday cash. Everyone will tell you that the euro crashed because of problems in Europe, which started with Greece. To appreciate what has been taking place, imagine yourself living in Greece, owning a few shares with your main savings being a lump of cash on deposit in the bank. TV tells you the country may default, i.e. go bust, that it may leave the euro, etc etc. As a sensible person, you do two things:

1. You change your bank and move to one outside the country - a British or American bank could be subject to local laws. You may end up in Germany or Denmark, where the bank pays you a negative rate of interest - you are paying the bank what amounts to an insurance premium.
2. You turn your cash out of euros into the strongest which is available, maybe US dollars or sterling. You know people who have moved into the Swiss franc and the Norwegian krone, but these are both small and restricted markets.

Thousands of people made these two simple decisions, which poured a mass of euros on to world currency markets. Euros behaved just like any other commodity - the price sank.

LOOK AT THE RATE

All this may happen again, or the euro might bounce back. So how do you manage your holiday money? There is one golden rule when you are buying currency: look at the rate. You need to ask the bank or bureau this one simple question:

What is your rate to sell me 500 euros? (or whatever)

You compare the replies you get and you choose the best, i.e. the one which gives you the largest number of euros or dollars. Buying a currency is just like buying a commodity, such as a pound of sugar or a pint of milk. Less common currencies, like rarer commodities, will be rather more expensive.

WATCH THE SPREAD

When you asked the bureau for the exchange rate, you made clear that you wanted to buy, not sell, euros. If you had wanted to sell, you would have been given a different, inferior rate(fewer euros for your pound) This is the bureau's 'spread' which is the difference between his buying price and his selling price. This is how he makes his money. The narrower the spread, the better for you.

When you buy euros, you may be told that the deal is commission-free. Just nod your thanks, and focus on the rate.

In theory, you should do better if the bureau does not charge a commission, but all you ever want to know is - how much are you going to get for your hard-earned pound sterling? Just how the man in the bureau fixes his dealing price has to be his concern, not yours.

USEFUL BUY BACK

One extra that might be useful is a guarantee, when you return from holiday, to buy back any unused currency at a similar rate to the one which you paid. This will give protection if you bring back a wad of euro notes and the rate moves against you - i.e. the euro reverses its decline, so that you get fewer pounds.

But in any case, the most sensible plan is to use up most of your euro notes while you are still abroad and keep any that are left over for your next trip. If you cash them in and draw euros again later, you will simply have paid the spread twice over!

LAST MINUTE COSTS

So you focus on the rate you get for your pounds. When should you buy your currency? You will probably get the worst rate if you buy all the euros you need at the last minute, when you get to the airport - unless you strike it lucky and buy just at the time the euro has gone into a nose-dive.

The sensible move is to spread your currency buying. If you are going away in six months' time, buy one third now, another third in three months and the rest shortly before you leave. This is what the stock market calls 'pound averaging.' Unless you decide to fix on a particular rate, this is the most practical way to cope with a fluctuating market.

USE THE NET

So where do you buy? You can buy your euros from your bank, from a travel agent or over the net. If you are keen to get the best rate (the differences can be significant) you need to spend some time checking around. The best rate will probably come over the net - and if you can collect the currency yourself from a bureau in central London. You download a voucher, go to the bureau with your cash and buy currency at the agreed rate. (You take cash because the bureau may not accept a credit card, and you may get charged by your bank if you use a debit card).

If you live outside a big town, or if personal collection is a problem, you can in most cases have the currency delivered. This will cost unless you put in a sizable order - probably a minimum of £500 or more. It makes sense to join with a friend so that the order will be delivered free. When the currency arrives, make certain that you have insurance cover either from a travel policy or under the contents section of your house insurance.

TAKING THE CURRENCY

So you have your currency and you are ready to go - but how will you get cash once you are abroad? Taking a large amount of cash is probably not the best idea: folding money can be lost or stolen. Travellers' cheques used to be the popular answer, and you can still buy them from American Express or Thomas Cook. You buy them in the currency you need, they are secure because they are numbered so can be replaced if lost or stolen. When you need cash abroad, you just take your travellers' cheques to a local bank and show some ID.

But there are two major snags to travellers' cheques. Overseas banks are liable to charge a heavy commission to give you cash for your cheque and the cash-in process is likely to be cumbersome. Secondly, you may well find that hotels and restaurants abroad are less than keen to take travellers' cheques. The locals do not use them and your hotel may also be hit by bank charges.

ATM COSTS

So you think hole-in-the-wall - get your cash from an ATM, just as you do in the UK. Good idea, so long as you work out the costs first. Getting cash from an ATM in Europe can be expensive, when you could be charged by the bank which issued your card and face a deduction by the ATM operator. There are just a few cards which avoid the double cost. As an alternative, you could open the right bank or building society account and use that debit card when you travel - that is effective, but cumbersome.

TRY A LOADED CARD

There is a simpler solution - use a loaded or prepaid card. Before you go, you buy your dollars or euros over the net or on the phone. These are loaded on to your card and when you go abroad you use the card in an ATM, or for shopping or in a restaurant. If you need extra cash, you can top up by making a phone call or over the net. Loaded cards are simple to get: as there is no credit, so no credit check and no bank is involved in your application.

CHECK THE CHARGES

One essential: you must check the charges on a loaded card. These vary a good deal - you may be charged to use the card in certain countries, or when you top up. (So it is best to be clear which countries you plan to visit). You could be charged when you close the card and you might have to pay an inactivity fee. You can budget with a loaded card and if it is stolen the thief cannot get into your bank account. You will not get any interest on the money which you load on to the card and you will not get the consumer protection which comes with a credit card.

AVOID THE COMMISSION

Most of your holiday spend will be on a credit card, where the rule is simple: use a card which does not charge a currency commission. Most credit cards(probably the one you use in the UK) will charge you an extra 2.5-3% when they turn a foreign spend into sterling which they log into your monthly statement. So you take a credit card issued by Halifax, Post Office, Nationwide, Santander or Saga (for the over 50s). You have to check the exact rules - some are commission-free in Europe, some are commission-free round the world. As with currencies, it helps if you know just where you are going to travel.

BIGGER DEALS NEED EXPERTS

You may be thinking of a bigger currency deal - maybe sending several thousand pounds to buy a time-share or pay the deposit on a flat. In that case, you will need expert advice, which means talking to a bank or a foreign exchange broker. Only a small difference in the currency exchange rate can have a significant impact on the cost in pounds sterling.

On any sizable deal, you should think about using the forward currency market.(When you deal today, you are operating in the spot market) When you have to find - or expect to receive - euros, dollars or whatever in say six months' time, you can fix today what that will amount to in pounds sterling.

You can fix a forward deal for anything from six months to two years, and this should not be a heavy cost. The difference between today's currency rate and what you arrange for the future will depend on relative interest rates - no one is going to make a forecast! For all this, you need expert help.

****

Chapter 5

Investing for Your 25 Years

Your objective is simple as you plan towards retirement - build up a pot of assets which you will be free to use as you wish - boost your pension, travel round the world, buy a sports car. You want the pot to grow over the years and you want to have easy access if you need it.

For most people, this means that you are looking at shares and unit trusts. Billionaire investors can buy entire companies through private equity deals, take over office buildings or they can stockpile physical commodities. As an average investor, you can go into property, though this comes in largish lumps and there is the question of access - can you cash in at a reasonable price and a reasonable speed when you want to? You may have special knowledge, of coins, stamps or fine wine but all the experts will tell you to limit exotic investments to 10-20% of your assets.

HOW MUCH RISK?

Your objective is clear, but you need to decide at an early stage how much risk you are prepared to face in getting there? If your assets will be important to help pay for your retirement, then you will look for low risk. If you have a financial cushion, say a generous pension scheme, then you can afford to take a higher risk profile. Bigger risk should bring a bigger reward, but there is no one who can actually make that happen. The first choice has to be between shares and fixed-interest. What you decide will depend largely on your age. When you invest, at age 45, you can take a long view and give companies time to come good. By age 55, five years from retirement, you do not want to take major risks with asset values. You start to think about the' lifestyle adjustment,' i.e. moving to safer fixed interest investments as you get older.

YOUR AGE IN BONDS.......

All this explains the old stock exchange rule - your age equals the percentage of your assets which you hold in bonds. As a one-sentence piece of investment advice, this rule is not bad. At age 35 you would be two-thirds in equities, while by age 55 you would be just over half in bonds.

The second choice has to be whether you buy specific shares and bonds or whether you stick to unit trusts. Unless you are wealthy or knowledgeable, the answer for most people is to stay with unit trusts. You will do much better if you buy the right shares (who bought Apple five years ago?) than with unit trusts - but finding the right shares is the toughest test of all. Companies can hit problems (think BP) and even big companies can go the way of the dinosaur. Look at any share index of a few years back and see how many names you still recognise - like ICI (bought by a European group), Woolworth (closed down).

........MAYBE RETAIL BONDS

Most people buy bonds though unit trusts, which give you a spread of risk and specialist help in a rather technical market.

Bond funds can be investment grade (the safest), higher yield (riskier) or strategic (the manager decides).

Now you can buy retail bonds direct, since the stock exchange changed its rules and brought the minimum deal down from £100,000 to £1,000. Tesco was one of the first to tap into this new market, followed by a firm of City dealers, a housing association and a finance group. You typically buy a bond yielding 5-6% with maturity in five or six years' time (if the bond has five years' life still left when you buy, you can shelter it in an ISA).

Retail bonds appeal because you know exactly where you are investing, when and how much interest is paid, when the bond is paid up and for how much. Bond funds appeal to people who want to spread their risk (a fund may hold anything up to 100 individual bonds) and funds - but not retail bonds - are covered by the Financial Services Compensation Scheme.

SAY YES TO SAYE

The one time you should buy shares is when you work for a public company which runs a SAYE scheme: Save As You Earn. (This is not a possible choice if you are self-employed or work for a private business). Essentially, the company issues shares at a discount - usually 20% - and you agree to save a fixed amount, up to £250 a month, for three or five years. You then have the option, to take the shares or walk away with the cash.

You can see the appeal - if the share price goes up, you take the shares, but if the share price goes down you take the cash. Workers at Tesco and Asda have gained from SAYE schemes over recent years. If you have a big gain, you can sell the shares (gains up to £10,600 are free of gains tax) or put them in an ISA.

RISK ELEMENT

There is one element of risk, if your employer goes bust. But even if the share price goes into free-fall, you still have the option to take cash.

There is another risk to SAYE - putting your eggs in one basket when you decide to keep the shares or put them in an ISA. This is why most individual investors go for unit trusts or 'pooled vehicles.' These just invest in particular assets - shares in the Far East, UK bonds, high-yield shares, whatever - and sell the units to investors. You spread your risk and you can choose active professional management.

TRUST OR FUND?

Nowadays you have an option, between traditional unit trusts and the newer Exchange Traded Funds. These two types do a similar job, but in different ways. ETFs are listed on the stock exchange, so investing is just like buying a share; unit trusts are sold by the fund manager. ETFs can borrow, which unit trusts cannot, so that good or bad results can be magnified. You will see ETFs labeled 'physical' or 'synthetic' while unit trusts are physical.

This terminology is confusing, because an ETF has the advantage that it can hold physical assets, such as gold or oil, which a unit trust may not do. A distinction is sometimes made between ET Funds, which track markets, ET Commodities, which follow commodity prices and ET Notes which can be linked to the price of almost any assets you care to think of. In this piece of jargon, physical means that the fund holds the assets; in a synthetic ETF, the fund does not hold assets but sets up contracts with banks which replicate the asset price. A synthetic ETF can have contracts on a whole variety of investments - though bringing in banks represents an extra risk. (Remember the Lehman crash?). ETFs tend to appeal to bigger, more active traders while unit trusts appeal more to the average investor.

ACTIVE OR PASSIVE?

Unit trust and ETF costs are similar, though in buying and selling ETFs you have to cost in stock exchange dealing, In unit trusts, the big cost issue is whether you choose active or passive management. In active management, you follow a particular fund manager, who will charge for his work. A typical actively managed fund will want 5% when you buy, plus a yearly total expense ratio of 1.5-2% (TER is the figure you should look at - mostly the management fee, plus incidentals such as registration work).

A passive fund, or tracker, is either a parcel of shares or a computer program. A passive fund which tracks say, the top 100 shares on the London stock exchange, will typically charge nothing at all when you buy and then 0.25% a year. (Some trackers charge more - you have to check before you invest).

LEADERS' LIST.....

So do you go active or passive? If you fancy a special sector or country, you will probably have to go active - like people attracted by investing in BRIC. (Brazil, Russia, India, China). You may also go active if the evidence points to a fund manager who can consistently outperform. Brokers will show you lists of 'leaders' who regularly beat the index.

Going passive will make a big saving on cost. If you are looking for 6% a year growth (the FSA's assumption, much better than the recent past!) an active fund will take a quarter in annual management costs and you will see virtually no growth at all in your first year.

......AND DOG FUNDS

If you look over the hundreds of active funds available, there is no doubt from UK and US data that a significant number fail to keep up with the stock market average - though the leaders and laggards are not always the same. The brokers who publish lists of leaders also publish lists of 'dog funds' - funds which are in the lowest quartile, or bottom 25%, of performance.

Some major fund managers have solved this dilemma by bringing out funds which are low-cost and actively managed. Schroders and JP Morgan have set up active funds where the TER (Total Expense Ratio) has been reduced to around 0.5% The Fidelity group operates active funds with TERs down to 0.9%. None of these funds carry any commission, so you can afford to buy direct from the manager.

CONTACT A DISCOUNT BROKER

Like many a sensible investor, you decide to buy some of each. You buy low-cost trackers which cover the UK and US markets and you pay more for actively managed funds which focus on sectors such as bonds, equity high income or specialist overseas markets. But there are ways to keep down the extra costs you have to pay for active management: you contact a discount broker. (Some people go direct to the fund manager - which simply means that they pay the full initial and annual charges)

A discount broker will give you useful cost savings, but he will not give you any advice. Your deal with him will be execution-only, which means that he only does what you tell him. To help you decide, some discount brokers provide information and research data, free of charge. Your deal will be handled via an investment platform, a kind of investment wholesaler where the discount broker is a customer - or he might have set up his own.

CASH FROM THE TRAIL

Discount brokers vary, but you can expect them to drop all or most of the initial charge, saving you a typical 5%. You should also get some saving on the annual charge, because the fund manager gives part of his management fee to the broker - known as 'trail commission' - so long as you stay invested. The discount broker will often give you some of this commission in order to keep your business.

Some discount brokers ask for a one-off fee and then give you all the trail commission. More generally, the discount broker will share his trail commission, and you should collect around 0.25% a year in cash as a sort of loyalty bonus.

Do not buy a tracker unit trust through a discount broker; this is when you can go direct. Trackers do not pay initial commission or trail commission - which is why they are so cost-effective. When fund managers do not pay trail commission on some unit trusts, you could even find the broker asking you for money to cover his expenses. (The Financial Services Authority grumbles about the payment of trail commission, and it might one day decide to outlaw the practice).

****

Chapter 6

Think About Re-mortgage

Your mortgage deal comes to an end, after two or three years, and you need to look for a new product. We are talking remortgage.

You could do nothing, when after the initial period you typically switch to your lender's Standard Variable Rate (SVR). If that rate looks attractive, it may not be worthwhile remortgaging. Nor will it be worth remortgaging if your mortgage has only a few years to go, or if it has run down to around £50,000 or less - the savings will simply not be big enough to meet the costs.

Assuming you want to go ahead, you have to check how much equity you hold in your property. This is the price which a valuer would put on the property, less the existing mortgage and any other debts which have been secured on your house.

TALK TO THE LENDER

Once you have settled this figure, one obvious first step could be to talk to your existing lender. He may not want to lose your business while getting a deal from him would save you a good deal of hassle and one-off spend. You should explore the alternatives before you remortgage, including taking a second mortgage from your existing lender. You may think of asking your lender to remortgage to a longer term, say to 30 years from your existing 25 years. Your monthly payments will fall, which is attractive - but there is a considerable drawback. You will pay much more in interest in total. You need to look at the figures over the whole 30 years as against 25 - many people just reckon on five years' extra interest, which can make the numbers look more appealing.

EQUITY NEEDED

The mortgage world has changed since the turmoil of 2007-8 - there are no more 125% mortgages, when you could borrow significantly more than your house was worth. To remortgage nowadays you will have to show equity of a minimum 20% - or face stiff interest rates.

One other change in the mortgage world will impact the self-employed - lenders' changing views of self-certification. In the early 2000s, it was possible for self-employed people to get mortgages by reporting on their own income. In today's more demanding times, lenders may ask for some independent support, say from your accountant.

SWAP FACILITY

For the over 55s, one new product is a mortgage/equity release swap. You take out an interest-only lifetime mortgage - you are still working and can afford to pay the interest. You like the cash flow advantage compared with a repayment mortgage and you are a few years young for the deal you would like on equity release. Later, when you retire and want to cut your outgoings, you can stop paying out interest and switch to a roll-up lifetime mortgage. This swap feature gives you flexibility and means that arrears will not be a problem.

Why do you want to re-mortgage? One typical answer is to pay a lower rate of interest, which could be a compelling reason if you are about to switch to an uncompetitive SVR. You may want to realise some of the equity in your house; you may want to wrap up other debts on loans or credit cards, or you may think of extending your home perhaps adding a conservatory.

KEEP UP LTV

You need to plan ahead and you may find that lenders react differently to different schemes. Typically, a lender would be happy with a minimum 20% equity - from his standpoint, an 80% LTV, loan to value - but might look for 40% equity if you just wanted to finance spending in general or consolidate short-term debts. This points one way to remortgage, when the value of your property has risen and your extra borrowing will simply maintain the existing Loan to Value.

When you start to look for your new remortgage product, you could feel overwhelmed by the sheer variety. For many people, the sensible reaction is to go and talk to a mortgage broker. But you are likely to have a more rewarding talk if you have some basic grasp of the remortgage products which are out in the marketplace. Here are some of the products you are likely to meet:

Capped rate: you agree a maximum above which the rate will not go, and you probably pay a slightly higher rate of interest on the mortgage. This represents an insurance against a spike in inflation and interest rates.

Cashback: the lender hands back some cash, useful for dealing with all the incidental expenses - especially if you are moving house. But you will probably have to return the cash if you want to leave the mortgage deal before it matures.

Collar rate: the lender may lay down a minimum below which the rate will not fall, whatever happens to base rate or other interest rates. Many lenders were caught unawares by the drop in interest rates which began five years ago, and rushed to set minimums below which they would not lend. (It is possible to arrange a mortgage which incorporates both a cap and collar, so that the rate can move only within a pre-determined range)

Discount: generally a discount on the lender's SVR, but you need to be very clear on how big a discount and on which rate. As with a cashback, you will probably face a penalty if you leave the mortgage early.

Fixed rate: the lender keeps the rate unchanged for an agreed number of years - you get certainty on your outgoings, which is of value in itself. A fixed rate will be important if the repayment costs stretch your budget, so you would be in difficulty at a sudden hike in interest rates. (Do not look backwards later to see if you were right to fix - hindsight rarely helps).

Tracker rate: the interest rate is set at a margin over Bank of England base rate, and probably represents borrowers' most popular choice. (A few years ago, you could have got a tracker rate below base rate). If you are very clever, you will know when to move between fixed rate and tracker (i.e. variable) rate borrowings. Interest rates' next move are expected to be up - but when and how much is not at all clear!

REDEMPTION QUOTE

So you decide to take the plunge and re-mortgage. The first step is to get a redemption quote from your current lender. It is essential that this includes any ERC - Early Redemption Charge -

and any discharge fee to which he is entitled (Check with your original borrowing agreement that he is entitled to make any charges he wants to impose.).

Next, you get a quotation from the new lender which you, or you and the broker, have identified. He will probably want an arrangement fee and you also have to budget for fees to the solicitor and the valuer. Some lenders are prepared to help towards these professional costs, though if the lender pays towards the legal costs you will probably have to use a solicitor he chooses to act for you. A mortgage broker will probably get his fee from the new lender - you need to confirm.

Before you sign, check - with the broker or the lender - how much you are going to save. Run the numbers over three years, five years and seven or 10. You need to know how with some precision much you will have to pay every month. You should also look at the new lender's SVR: if you choose a cashback or discount deal, this is the rate you will be paying when your deal comes to an end. And it is worth comparing his SVR with other lenders to see how he rates in the marketplace.

REPAY - OR NOT?

One fundamental mortgage choice - whether you go interest-only is an option for people of pension age, but may now be problematic for younger borrowers. An interest-only mortgage means just what it says: you just pay interest on the amount you have borrowed. With a traditional mortgage, your monthly payment involves two things - an interest payment plus a repayment of capital.

An interest-only mortgage means that your current outgoings are that much less - but at the end of the mortgage you still have your debt to pay. Your cautious neighbour, who took a traditional mortgage, suffered more financial pain on the way but ended his mortgage term entirely debt-free.

HOUSE PRICES AHEAD?

The case for choosing an interest-only mortgage used to be that rising house prices over 20-30 years would clear the debt. You would then sell your house or remortgage. Post-squeeze, this prospect looks less certain (average house prices rose 2-3% over the past year) so that both lenders and borrowers have started to hold back on this type of deal. Whitehall has also started to worry over the numbers of people who hold significant amounts of debt on interest-only mortgages.

An interest-only mortgage will still make sense if cash flow is important to you for a few years, when you can then switch to a traditional repayment mortgage. It will also make sense if you can see an extra source of income coming a few years ahead - maybe your partner plans to go back to work when the children are older, maybe you expect to inherit.

THINK OFFSET?

For people who have built up some savings - and especially if they are higher rate taxpayers - a switch to an offset mortgage has considerable appeal. Suppose that you are a 40% taxpayer, you have a mortgage of £120,000 while you and your partner have built up savings of £30,000, invested with a bank or building society.

This is no way an optimum financial situation. You pay a higher interest rate on your mortgage than you get from the bank. You pay tax on the interest from your savings, but there is no tax relief on the interest you pay your mortgage lender.

So you go to your mortgage lender and agree an offset mortgage. This means that you offset your savings against your debt and pay interest on £90,000 - you have cut your monthly bill by a quarter. You have lost the after-tax interest on your savings and the offset mortgage may cost a little more, but the 25% interest saving leaves you well ahead. Cutting your interest payments is the key to the deal, so you will need to have savings of at least £25,000 - and significant in relation to your mortgage - in order to make the numbers work.

LOOK EVERY YEAR

Remortgaging can make you significant amounts of money, so it is worth looking at your mortgage (and house value) every year to see whether a deal makes sense. There are one-off legal and valuation costs whenever you remortgage, but you should be able to get some help from the new lender.

If the numbers look good, remember that you are free to remortgage as many times as you like!

****

Chapter 7

Pay Less Income Tax

From January 1 to April or May every year, many of us work for the government. That is the proportion of our income for the 12 months which we pay over in tax. That is just income tax - not even including VAT - and you are also liable to pay capital gains tax when you sell shares or unit trusts. When you die, you may leave behind a bill for inheritance tax which your family will have to pay. No wonder people ponder ways to reduce their tax bill.

When you think about paying less income tax, the first point to take on board is that Her Majesty's Revenue and Customs (HMRC) make mistakes which can leave you out of pocket. Over the recent past, they have lost taxpayers' records, made over-payments on tax credits and issued incorrect demands for further tax - early in 2012 up to 1.6 million people received a tax demand for over £500 after they were charged the wrong amount. The taxman is not infallible.

KEEP HMRC UP TO SPEED

This means that you have to stay alert: this is just between you and HMRC, unless you hire an accountant or a financial adviser. You need to give HMRC all the key data about yourself and your family and - this is especially important - keep them up to speed whenever there is any change. Tell them if you get a new job, move house, or when a new baby arrives.

You need to keep records, going back at least six years. You have a legal obligation, but you will also need records if HMRC slips up and to make sure you are getting all the reliefs you should. A survey this summer found that three out of five higher-rate taxpayers admitted they were not claiming full relief on their pension contributions and one out of five did not even know whether they were claiming or not. Do not follow that example!

READ WHAT THEY SEND

HMRC will write to you and it is important that you read their letters. Early in the year they will send you a notice of coding, which tells your employer how much tax to take out of your wages. Check the HMRC figures, especially carefully if your tax situation has changed over the previous 12 months - you got a new company car, paid more into a pension, or made a donation to charity.

All this is fine, you say, but people also need to be pro-active and take the initiative on tax -saving. That is100% correct - so here are some initiatives.

A. BE A ONE- MAN COMPANY

See who forms a one-man, personal service, limited company in order to be tax-efficient - a top civil servant who saved £40,000 a year, BBC presenters and newsreaders, Boris Johnson and Ken Livingstone, as disclosed when they competed to be Mayor of London. This is what you do:
- Form a company - you can buy one off the shelf - and make yourself director (add your partner if they do not pay tax);

- Agree a contract with your employer, so that he pays the company;
- The company is liable for corporation tax at 20% and you pay yourself a salary equal to the tax-free personal allowance - £8,105 for 2012-13;
- You pay yourself dividends which are effectively tax-free (20% corporation tax has already been paid) up to the higher rate band, which kicks in from £34,371; (you also realise that you have avoided paying National Insurance);
- When you want to access the cash which has accumulated, maybe some years later, you wind up the company.

A higher-rate taxpayer will see his income fall until he accesses the cash. But apart from the significant tax savings, there are side benefits - with your new minimal income you could claim tax credits and child benefit.

Operating this type of company successfully needs to involve an adviser - you cannot just switch from being a full-time employee to a one-man company, and there are jobs for which these companies do not fit. Some advisers will tell you to wait until you move to a new employer before setting up your personal service company.

One-man companies work most easily when you draw income from several sources. Think of a leading footballer who is also paid for sponsorship and for after-dinner speaking.

There are reckoned to be around half a million one-man personal service limited companies operating in the UK. If you think that you fit the profile, the tax potential is well worth exploring.

B. CHECK WITH YOUR PARTNER

The odds are that you and your partner pay tax at different rates - they may have a better job than you, or she has temporarily given up work to look after the young children. Whatever the set-up, the tax-saving rule is simple.

The partner with the lower tax rate holds the bank deposits, shares and unit trusts, while the partner with the high tax rate pays into pension funds and donates to charity. (Warning: if you are a non-taxpayer who donates to charity, tell the charity not to make a claim on HMRC - otherwise the taxman will want the money back from you!)

Moving the ownership of shares or unit trusts is easy - you just download a stock transfer form over the net and send it to the company registrar. Transfers between married couples and civil partners are free from capital gains tax, so no liabilities arise. This is emphatically not true for transfers between unmarried partners, who have no connection in the eyes of HMRC.

In that case, a transfer represents a sale which could mean that you pay gains tax - unless you operate within your annual exemption or have offsetting losses. Transfers of cash and bank deposits do not raise any gains tax issues.

Some people may have reservations about handing over all their share and unit trust holdings. Joint ownership represents a compromise solution - moving to joint names involves the same transfer procedure with the registrar. The taxman will assume that joint ownership means a 50-50 split, unless you tell him otherwise.

Gains tax liabilities will then be shared equally between you as will dividend and interest income, so that the income tax bill comes down. When you choose joint ownership, set up a joint bank account for the income which arises.

Joint ownership has a useful side benefit at the time one of you dies. When that happens, all assets which are jointly owned immediately become the property of the other holder. You do not have to wait for probate on the estate, which can cause delays at a difficult time.

C. THINK SALARY EXCHANGE

Salary exchange - formerly called salary sacrifice - is a simple way to save money which would otherwise go in tax and National Insurance. In the basic salary exchange scheme, you exchange part of your salary for a non-cash benefit, such as when your employer pays an agreed amount into your pension fund.

Suppose you exchange £100 of salary which the employer pays into your pension pot. You save NI of either 1% or 11% and your income tax bill also comes down. (You could be better off with a lower salary if you are getting working tax credit or child tax credit). Your employer saves NI at 12.8% and his wage bill also comes down.

Salary exchange need not affect salary-linked benefits, e.g. life assurance. If that arises, the benefits will be calculated using your 'reference salary' - effectively the salary before salary exchange. Pensions are a popular outlet for salary exchange, but there is now a sizable menu of alternatives. Your employer may provide childcare vouchers or offer you longer holidays. Some companies will arrange for lower-price cars or cycles and some schemes offer savings in health screening and local car parking.

Salary exchange can become especially appealing when you approach one of the tipping points in the tax system - where, if you do nothing, you suddenly find yourself paying a sharply higher rate of tax. One tipping point is the shift from the standard 20% rate to the higher 40% rate, which happens at £34,371 in the 2012-13 financial year. Another comes at £100,000, when HMRC starts to withdraw your personal allowance - £1 for every £2 of income above that level, so that your marginal tax rate shoots up to a painful 62%.

D. TALK TO YOUR EMPLOYER

Benefiting from salary exchange is one of the advantages of being an employee - as opposed to having to negotiate direct with HMRC. The other great advantage of being an employee is that you can access the company's pension fund - which, over the next few years, all companies will have to provide and finance. The employer contributes to the fund, whether it is defined benefit (=final salary, rare nowadays for new entrants) or defined contribution(=money purchase), so this is a no-brainer. If you do not join, you are passing up a potentially significant amount of cash which your employer provides for the benefit of your retirement (this is the simple reason why pensions are so often better than ISAs - see Chapter 2).

But there is a whole range of other tax-efficient benefits which are open to you as an employee - you might have to ask. If you work for a financial business, you could have an interest-free loan up to £5,000 without this being treated as a taxable benefit. If you have to work from home, your employer can pay you a small amount without keeping any records - more if there is written back-up. Your employer can provide you with a mobile phone which you can use privately and he can arrange medical check-ups for you or your family. Talk to your colleagues and discuss with HR.

E. FIND A LODGER - TAX-FREE

If you let a furnished room to a lodger, the first £4,250 a year, equal to £350 a month, comes free of tax under the Rent a Room scheme. The room must be in the main place where you live, and the scheme applies to people who rent their home as well as to owners. Think of Rent a Room when junior goes off to university, and rents a flat or house where there is space to sublet.

Rent a room does not apply to offices but does include lodgers who study at home or people who do some of their business work from home. If you offer cleaning or laundry, that will be included in the £4,250 a year.

The scheme is simple - you just log the rent you receive and expenses are ignored. If you get more than £4,250 a year, you have a choice. You can simply pay tax on the excess or you can opt for the usual route - deduct expenses from income and pay tax on the net receipts.

Suppose that you let for £7,000 a year and your costs plus capital allowances amount to £4.000. Under the first route (Rent a Room) you would pay tax on £2,750 (£7,000 minus £4,250). On the second route (income less expenses) your taxable income would be £3,000, (£7,000 minus £4,000) so slightly less attractive.

If you own the house, letting a room to a lodger will not cut across the exemption from gains tax when you come to sell - so long as you have just one lodger. HMRC will accept one lodger, but two or more means to them that you are running a business.

When you work this scheme at university, one of junior's friends living in the same property could also operate Rent a Room. Two people can run Rent a Room in the same house, though the tax-free amount is halved to £2,125.

F. THINK OFFSHORE

Offshore bonds are a useful way to defer tax, especially if you expect to go down the tax scale when you retire. The key feature of offshore bonds is your ability to withdraw up to 5% of your investment, free of immediate tax, every year for 20 years.

You can choose when to pay tax - say cashing in your bond when you move from paying higher rate tax to standard rate. Offshore bonds themselves are more tax-efficient than OEICs and unit trusts, which are their onshore equivalent. An onshore portfolio is taxed annually, but funds held within offshore bonds can grow free of year-on-year taxation.

BUT WHEN AN INSPECTOR CALLS.......

You have your tax sorted, you carefully check all the figures you send the Inspector - then one day HMRC tells you that it has started an inquiry into your tax affairs for a certain year. You have to send them copies of all your bank statements plus a file of other records.

After the initial shock, your first question is: why me? Probably, your case was chosen at random. If not, HMRC may suspect that you have a source of income which you have not declared - in that case the Inspector is liable to become persistent and may launch another inquiry later on.

You will probably need help from an accountant, but you can offset the costs against your pre-tax income - unless the Inspector finds somewhere where you have underpaid tax. If you are worried about an inquiry and the possible costs, it is possible to take out insurance.

PS - WAITING FOR 6 APRIL 2013

Top rate taxpayers know that their 50% rate comes down to 45% from 6 April 2013. The top tax rate on dividends comes down at the same time from 42.5% to 37.5% - so the Treasury should expect that whenever people can, they will defer salaries, bonuses and dividends from 2012-13 to 2013-14. Pension contributions will be made in 2012-13 rather than 2013-14, to get relief at £500 per £1,000 rather than £450. All this is a no-brainer, but there is one small snag. If deferral means that your income falls between £100,000 and £118,410 you will pay a marginal tax rate of 62%. Avoid that.

****

Chapter 8

Facing the Other Big Taxes

Everyone's big tax bill is for income tax, but over the years to come you expect to have to pay Capital Gains Tax (CGT). One day, your family will be hit by Inheritance Tax (IHT) on your estate.

You make a capital gain when you sell or give away an asset for more than you paid. Most capital gains mean that you will have to pay CGT, but there is a range of concessions. You get an annual exemption - for the first £10,600 of your gains in the 2012-13 financial year.

18%/28%

If your gains go above the exempt level, you pay CGT at 18% when your gains and income together total less than £34,370, which is the upper limit for standard rate tax. Above that limit, you pay CGT at 28%. Trustees pay the higher rate; entrepreneurs who are selling their own business pay 10%.

When you give an asset to your spouse or civil partner, that does not count as a disposal for CGT. But note: when they come to sell your gift, they take over your original acquisition date - not the date when you gave it to them. Each spouse has their own annual exemption, so that when you sell a jointly owned asset you will only pay CGT when the gain goes over £21,200.

HOME FREE

Selling your home (principal private residence in the taxman's jargon) is free from CGT - which is why some people never pay the tax. Nor do you pay CGT when you sell your car or personal belongings (chattels). ISAs are free from CGT, along with anything you win from betting, the lottery or football pools. Many people first encounter CGT when they make a healthy profit from selling shares or unit trusts - either planned or following a take-over. When you see that deal coming, make sure that the shares are held in joint names with your partner, so that your annual exemption is doubled.

USE IT OR LOSE IT

This £10,600 exemption does not carry over from year to year. You use it or lose it! This points to a key way to avoid CGT - make full use of your annual allowance. Suppose that you have a holding of unit trusts, which are worth more than you paid for them. The assumption has to be that one day you may want to sell. When that day comes, you will want the cost to be close to the market value, in order to minimise the amount of gains tax you will have to pay. So every year you sell part of your holding, making sure that the gains stay inside the £10,600 exemption - and then you buy back the number of units which you have sold. After a few years, the cost and the market value of your investment will become very close.

B&B UP TO DATE

This used to be a simple procedure, known as 'bed and breakfast' but the last Labour government brought in a new rule - that you

74

had to wait 30 days before buying back. That means that you face a market risk, as prices could move against you in the interim. You can simply wait out the time, but there are other options:

Bed and Spouse: you sell your shares or units, and immediately your spouse buys the same type and number;

Bed and ISA: you sell and immediately buy the units from a stocks and shares ISA - which you have to do if you wanted to transfer the units into an ISA;

Bed and SIPP: use your self-invested pension plan in the same way as an ISA;

Switch: sell and immediately buy a clone investment - if you sold an M&G tracker of the London stock market, buy a HSBC tracker.

WHEN TO LOOK FOR A LOSS

You may be put in the most difficult situation of all - you have investments which stand well above cost when a sudden crisis means that you need a large piece of cash. The first step is to check whether you or your spouse have any assets which are showing a loss on what you paid. You can realise these losses and aim to reduce your gains to the exemption level, £10,600 for each of you and £21,200 jointly.

As an alternative, try not to sell - or at least move part of your sale into the next financial year, when you will have a fresh exemption amount. Only sell as a last resort - if you need cash and hold investments which stand above cost, try for a secured loan or overdraft from your bank. As your investments have done well, they will probably be good and marketable securities.

YOU HAVE TO TAKE CASH

Aside from your suddenly needing cash, this gains tax issue will arise when your investment is turned into cash - whether you like it or not. You may hold shares for which another company makes a take-over bid in cash, probably from outside the UK. You read about the take-over in the newspaper and after a week or two the formal documents arrive. You will have at least three weeks in which to take the cash (that is the law) and the offer may be extended.

But at that point you need to accept - otherwise you may be left with an investment which is not readily marketable and may no longer even be listed. If all this happens in the early months of the financial year, the best you can do is make sure the shares are registered in joint names and realise any losses which you may hold.

WHEN A TRUST CLOSES

The same issue can arise when you hold unit trusts - you get a letter from the fund manager telling you that your fund will be merged with another one, or closed down because it is no longer economic to operate. If you are lucky, the manager will allow you to swap into another fund. If that happens, there should not be any CGT issues. Instead of 100 shares in Fund A you will simply hold 150 shares(or whatever) in Fund B; all the cost and ownership data stay the same. In any take-over, an exchange of shares does not create a CGT liability. But nowadays the fund manager will often tell you that your fund is being wound up - the banks have become keen to tidy up their outside business. All the trust's assets will then be sold and the cash handed out to unit holders. In that case, you are in the same position as a shareholder who faces a cash take-over. The taxman will not cut you any slack because the cash was in effect imposed on you. In his eyes, you disposed of the units, so you pay the CGT.

CGT ON SECOND HOMES

In recent years, when stock markets have been performing poorly, not so many people have had to pay CGT bills from selling shares or unit trusts - their gains have stayed inside the exemption limits. But people have been facing CGT when they wanted to sell second homes or holiday flats, especially in areas of higher prices such as London and the south-east. The amounts involved can be large - but there are some ingenious ways to avoid or reduce how much tax you have to pay. You buy your house and after a few years you decide that a holiday flat would be a good idea. You know that selling your main home would be free from CGT. But when you come to sell your holiday flat, you appreciate that you are liable to pay CGT on the profit - 28%, just over a quarter, of your gain will go to the taxman. So you look for an alternative.

ELECTION NEEDED

Once you buy your holiday flat, your first important task is to write to HMRC and tell them which property you have decided ('elected' in the taxman's jargon) is your main home. You have a two year window. If for some reason you do not make a decision, the taxman will decide for you, based on the facts of the situation. Be aware - it is important that you write to HMRC within the two years. Once you have made your election, you can change that election at any time in favour of any other property.

That opens the way for "flipping," an entirely legal tax planning arrangement - carried out by MPs in the last Parliament, including the then Chancellor of the Exchequer - which can bring big savings. Here is how flipping works:

- You tell HMRC that your house is your main home, so keeping its tax-free status;
- After a couple of years, you get an offer for your holiday flat which you cannot refuse;
- A week before the flat is sold, you write to HMRC telling them to flip your main home to the holiday flat;
- After the sale, you write again to HMRC telling them to flip your main home back to the house;
- Now comes the punch-line: because the flat was your main home, even for just a week or so, you benefit from the 'time to sell' rules. When a property has been your main home, for any period, the taxman will ignore the rise in value over the last three years. So because you flipped, and your holiday flat became - even briefly - your main home, it enjoyed tax-free status for the whole time you owned it - less than three years. Your house will lose its 'main home' relief for a few days, but that should not amount to a large total, especially if you are a long-term owner.

RESULT: YOU SELL YOUR HOLIDAY FLAT/SECOND HOME AT A HANDSOME PROFIT AND DO NOT PAY A PENNY OF CGT.

You can flip a holiday flat or a second home at any time - and save tax - but the real benefit comes when you buy and sell the flipped property within three years. That way, you escape CGT completely.

You can carry on flipping, as some MPS did, but you have to be realistic. When you tell HMRC that a property is your main home, it helps if the local authority know, as well as the post office and your telephone and utility suppliers.

****

Chapter 9

Inheritance Tax

Inheritance tax (IHT) which is paid on what you leave in your will, looks simple in theory. The taxman ignores the first £325,000 of your estate - this is the 'nil rate band.' Above that band, he charges tax at 40%. (This nil rate band has been fixed until 2015-16, after then it will be index-linked).

Suppose your estate turns out to be worth £375,000 - after taking out debts such as mortgages and outstanding bills. The excess is £50,000 so that the IHT amounts to £20,000. For many people, the biggest item in their estate will be the house they lived in - and there are reckoned to be 600,000 houses and flats which are worth more than the £325,000 nil rate.

WORLD-WIDE COVER

The taxman will charge IHT on your assets anywhere in the world (unless you are an overseas tax resident)and he will include investments like ISA's which were previously tax-free. He will also include any gifts you made over the previous seven years, unless these were exempt from IHT. (A gift is known as a 'potentially exempt transfer' - it will potentially be caught for some IHT unless you live for another seven years). A gift becomes entirely tax-free if you live for another seven years, so the taxman operates a sliding scale. If the gift was made 3-4 years before death, he adds 80% of its value. For 4-5 years, he adds

60%, for 5-6 years 40% and 6-7 years 20%. Whenever you make a gift, it is a good idea to confirm in a letter.

EXEMPT TO SPOUSE.......

Maybe you skilfully made some IHT-exempt gifts - these will not be added to the estate even if you die within seven years. Most important of these are any gifts made to your spouse or civil partner, even if you do not live together. (this exemption ends if you divorce) Unmarried partners do not have this benefit. Also exempt are gifts you made up to £3,000 in any tax year, which can be carried forward for one more year. (Spouses and civil partners each have the £3,000 allowance). You can also give £250 each year to any number of different people provided they have not received any other gifts from you.

AND FOR A WEDDING

Wedding gifts are also exempt (up to £5,000 for each parent, £2,500 for each grandparent and £1,000 for anyone else) as is money spent on your child's education up to age 18. One potentially useful exemption covers any gifts which you make out of income and do not affect your standard of living - i.e. you do not have to draw on capital. It helps if these gifts are made on a regular basis - say payments by covenant to an insurance policy which could be written in trust. You may need advice to decide what does not affect your standard of living.

HELP FOR CHARITIES

One recent concession on IHT aims to help charities. You will save 10% on your IHT bill - reducing the rate from 40% to 36%

- if you leave 10% of your estate to a charity, or to an amateur sports club.

Shares on AIM are exempt from IHT, provided you have held them for at least two years. Also exempt are assets of non-incorporated businesses, controlling shareholdings and owner-occupied farms - but in this area you will need specialist advice.

USE THE NIL RATE BAND

So how do you keep down the bill for IHT? The first step is to use the nil rate band, currently £325,000. The last Labour government brought in a concession, so that spouses and civil partners could take over any allowances which their partner had not fully used - and this concession was backdated.

Say that a widow realises her husband, who died two years ago, did not use £75,000 of his nil rate band. She can add that £75,000 to her own nil rate band of £325,000 - the extra £75,000 equal to a saving of £30,000 in hard cash.

SPOUSES - BUT NOT RELATIVES

Making full use of only partly used IHT allowances is useful - but with two qualifications. One is that it applies only to spouses and civil partners. Unmarried partners do not benefit, nor do relatives who live together. (Two elderly sisters who shared a house tried to claim the benefit, but lost).

The second qualification is that, when you claim under backdating, you will have to prove your case to HMRC. You will need documentation, such as the deed of probate and the death certificate - not always easy to find after some years.

WHEN YOU PAY NO IHT

All this points to a simple formula for the will. Suppose that the set-up involves a spouse and two children and only those three will inherit. The nil rate band of £325,000 is left to the children and everything else goes to the spouse. No IHT need be paid, because the children's inheritance falls within the tax-free nil rate band and there is no IHT on leaving money to a spouse.

An alternative would be to leave everything to the spouse - so that the children would inherit later, when the surviving spouse dies. The survivor's estate would be bigger, but that would be offset by the doubling of their IHT-free allowance to £650,000.

MAKE A WILL.

That family set-up is straightforward, but many are more complex. The moral: it is essential to make a will. Making a will is the only way to direct where your assets will go. When someone dies without making a will, the rules of intestacy apply. These could mean that part of your estate goes to people you did not intend to benefit and might even result in paying more IHT. (in the extreme case, with no will and no relatives, all your estate could go the Crown!).

To make a will, go to a solicitor - the cost is not huge, and there has to be a greater risk of challenge to a DIY will. For unmarried partners, it is important that they each make a will - remember that in the eyes of HMRC, unmarried partners have no connection unless one of them can show financial dependence.

HOW DO YOU OWN THE HOUSE?

Probably the most important part of the will is where it lays down what happens to the house. That will also depend on how the two partners own it. Most people are joint tenants - when the first one dies, the house goes to the second. But it is also possible for the partners to own the house as tenants in common.

This means that each partner owns a separate 50% of the house (or any other percentage, which you tell the taxman). Each partner is then free to leave their 50% to whoever they choose - which can have potential IHT advantages, depending on the total family set-up. Creating tenants in common could also be useful if one partner has to go into long-term care.

DEBT OR GIVEAWAY?

Reducing the IHT bill comes down to a simple activity - you part with assets. You can do this in one of two ways, by creating debt or giving the assets away. To create debt, you could just take out a £50,000 mortgage or loan, hand out cash to the beneficiaries - and make sure that you live for at least another three years. If you manage a total of seven years, the cash gifts become totally exempt and your estate for IHT has been reduced by the full £50,000. As the IHT tax rate is 40%, you will have saved £20,000 cash.

Cutting liability for IHT if often seen as a side-benefit of equity release, as the value of the estate is reduced by the amount of debt which has been created (see the next chapter). With a lifetime mortgage, the debt equals the loan capital plus rolled-up interest. With a home reversion plan, you have sold off part or all of your house.

A GIFT MUST BE A GIFT

Giving assets away, i.e. gifting them, looks the simplest of all - but there is an important catch. The gift must be entirely genuine (an 'absolute gift' in the jargon) which means no conditions, no understandings and nothing in return. If there are strings attached, the taxman will call it a gift 'with reservation' and just ignore the gift when he does his calculations for IHT. When you give your daughter the family's holiday flat, you must operate totally at arm's length - which means paying her a proper market rent whenever you go to stay.

Taking on debt and giving away assets will reduce the IHT which will have to be paid on your estate - but there is an obvious practical question. You cannot know with certainty how much debt to create nor how much money to give away, because you do not know what you are going to need for the rest of your life. You may also have issues about giving assets away to people you think cannot handle money or might get involved in divorce.

TRUST IN TRUSTS?

So you think about Trusts, acceptable to HMRC, which allow you to give away assets while keeping some access to income and/or capital. You will need professional advice, but setting up a trust could be sensible if you own a significant amount of assets or if your affairs are at all complex. Two well-known types of trust are:

- Loan Trust (straightforward): you make a small gift to set up the trust and then provide an interest-free loan which the trustees invest. All the growth in that investment arises within the trust, therefore outside your estate. The original loan can be repaid at any time, giving you what amounts to income - or a series of lump sum repayments.
- Discounted Gift Trust (more complex): you make a gift into an insurance bond, fixing how much income you take for the rest of your life. After seven years, the bond will not count as part of your estate. Even if you die within seven years, there should be an IHT saving because your right to an income discounts the value of your gift.

The size of the discount depends on your age, health and how much income you take - the older and less healthy you are, the smaller the discount. HMRC have counter-attacked this type of planning, arguing in one recent case that the heirs of a 90-year old were entitled to only a very small discount.

TWO YEARS TO CHANGE

The first, maybe the only, time you come across IHT yourself is when you inherit from someone's estate. You may be surprised at the lack of planning for future IHT, so you think 'deed of variation.'

Under a deed of variation, you can go to court and re-write someone's will within two years of their death - provided that everyone who stands to benefit agrees with your plans.(It becomes more complicated if children are involved) You will need legal advice, but the benefits could be significant.

You could save future tax by moving bequests from grown-up children to grandchildren. So long as he gets his IHT, the taxman has no interest in who are the beneficiaries. This ability to arrange future savings is why experts have long been expecting the government to end the flexibility offered by deeds of variation.

****

Chapter 10

Money From the House

For many people in the 50 plus generation, life can be cash poor though asset rich. We are all living longer, while inflation hurts and savings rates are the lowest for years. The only serious amount of cash you can find - cash which you can use any way you want - lies in the house where you live.

There used to be a traditional pattern of events - the kids grew up, then left home leaving you and your partner with a house that was too large. So you sold, making a profit which was free of capital gains tax, and moved to a smaller property.

WHY MOVE?

But life has changed. The kids may still live at home because they cannot get on to the property ladder. You and your partner may not want to move, you know the house and you like the neighbourhood. Moving is a hassle, and is not cheap - buying a £300,000 house will cost you £9,000 in stamp duty alone.

You could mortgage, maybe take an interest-only mortgage. That would be a help, but you will have the drain of having to make regular monthly interest payments. There is an alternative - equity release. This means just what it says, that you get your hands on the equity in your house, i.e. what it is worth over and above a mortgage or any other debt. You stay in your own home, and with a lifetime mortgage you are still the owner.

OLDER IS BETTER

To access equity release, you and your partner should be in your 50s and 60s - older people get better terms. Your house should be worth at least £75,000 with no unusual features or problems. Equity release will be simpler if you live in England and Wales.

There are no tax issues on money released from the value of your home it's yours to spend as you please - nor will your pension be affected. (Equity release is supervised by the Financial Services Authority). You need to own your own home, so that if there is an outstanding mortgage that will be wrapped up in the amount you raise on equity release.

NO INTEREST TO PAY OUT

The most popular type of equity release is a Lifetime mortgage, which will give you between 25% and 40% of your home's present-day value, depending on your age. This is like any other mortgage, but with one crucial difference - you do not pay out any money by way of interest, as the payments are rolled up until you (or both of you) die or go into long-term care.

You continue to own your home, as with any other mortgage. You will probably be given the option of taking a lump sum or draw down a series of payments, which will mean lower interest costs. Or you can agree a pre-arranged amount and make drawings up to that limit.

With a lifetime mortgage, you can expect to get a 'no negative equity' guarantee. This is important, because if you live into your 90s the rolled-up interest will pile up, and house prices may fall. But the guarantee means that your family will not have to cover any shortfall in debt.

COMPOUND INTEREST HITS

When you start to think about equity release, you could buy a book of compound interest tables - and see how a debt of £20,000 costing 6% trebles to just over £60,000 in 20 years. Interest rates are higher on lifetime than on normal mortgages, because lenders are committing to the long-term.

The no-negative equity guarantee points to the first thing to do when you think equity release - talk to the family. Equity release creates a debt which means that your estate will be that much smaller (so less IHT to pay) and, later on, the house itself will be sold. You need to plan ahead what you will do with the cash you get from equity release. It is sensible to make some estimate of how big the lifetime mortgage is likely to grow.

WHEN YOU MOVE

You should think carefully about equity release, and view it as a lifetime commitment. You may be able to unwind the arrangements at a later stage, but that is likely to be complex and will cost. You should be free to move house, but there may be issues if the value of the new house is very different from your present one - with a lifetime mortgage, you may have to repay part of the loan if you move to a lower value property

Do not forget the law of unintended consequences. Equity release will give you a lump of cash, or a series of lumps, from which you will draw dividends and interest. That could affect means-tested benefits and grants which you get from the state or a local authority. The extra income could also impact your tax position, say by reducing your age allowance. All of this needs to be worked out before you sign up.

CHECK OUT COSTS

Finally, before going ahead, you need to check out the costs. These vary a good deal among lenders - some charge no upfront fees, while others could cost you £2,000 or more. (It may be possible to add some costs to the amount of the loan). The lender may ask for an application or arrangement fee. The firm which values your house will also want a fee, which the lender may pay - or not.

It is probably best that you have your own lawyer, and some lenders will give you a fixed amount to help towards that fee. You may feel that you want expert advice, say from an independent financial adviser who has experience in equity release, and that advice will cost. The whole process should take between six and eight weeks.

OR HOME REVERSION?

If you have doubts about the lifetime mortgage type of equity release (maybe you are convinced that you will live to a very ripe old age and so push up the interest cost)think about the alternative, which is home reversion. In home reversion you sell a part of your house for cash - up to 100%. You may be able to start with a low percentage and sell more at a later stage. Depending on your age, the amount of cash you get will represent a significant discount on the house's market value because the lender can only take over ownership when you (or both of you) have died or gone into long-term care. The minimum age for home reversion is generally 65 (you and your partner) against 55 for a lifetime mortgage.

YOU ARE A TENANT - RENT-FREE

Under home reversion, you become a tenant who will pay no, or nominal, rent. You agree to insure the house and keep it in good condition. The house will be sold in due course, but if you sell 50% you ensure that the remaining 50% stays in your estate for the benefit of your family - though you can only guess what that is likely to be worth. Once you have set up a home reversion scheme, it may not be easy to cancel. You do not have to worry about interest accruing over the years, as you would with a lifetime mortgage. Your gain will be limited if house prices rise, as the lender gets the gain on the 50% or whatever which he has bought. With a lifetime mortgage, you remain the owner of the house, so you get all the benefit if prices rise. If house prices fall, you are better off with home reversion - the price drop on the share you sold becomes the lender's problem, not yours.

One caution on home reversion: if you die or go into care soon after starting a plan, you could have sold part of your home cheaply. Some schemes offer rebates if that happens, or you can look into insurance.

BOTTOM LINE: if you need more cash, and do not want to move house, equity release can be a good answer.

Chapter 11

Paying For University

Since September 2012, a university student taking out the maximum loans for tuition fees and maintenance costs will be looking at a debt of around £50,000 when they graduate - serious money, maybe just at the time they are starting to think about getting on the property ladder.

We all know that universities have been allowed to raise tuition fees up to £9,000 a year, and that three out of four are charging the maximum. Less widely known is that the repayment rules for student loans have also changed and that students are now being charged a higher rate of interest to finance their borrowing.

All students can get a tuition fee loan up to £9,000 a year. Students can also apply for a maintenance loan - partly means-tested and depending on the course - ranging from £4,375 if they live at home up to £7,675 living away from home and studying in London.

EARLY START

If you think that junior might go to university - as do about half the teenagers in the country - it is almost never too early to begin financial planning. A good starting point is the junior ISA (see the ISA chapter) where £3,600 can be invested each year completely free of income tax and gains tax - including for parents who set them up. Where children already have Child

Trust Funds, family and friends can pay in up to £3,600 a year and any interest comes tax free.

When children reach age 16 they can subscribe to a cash ISA, but under 18s are not eligible for a stocks and shares ISA. A danger lurks here - if the child gets more than £100 a year gross (as opposed to non-taxable) income from funds which the parent provided, then that income is assessed on the parent.

USE THEIR ALLOWANCES

Always remember that children have their own allowances on income tax and capital gains tax - just like the grown ups. One way to make use of these allowances is to set up a bare trust (relatively easy to do) where assets are held by a trustee for the child's benefit. HMRC will treat the income as if it belonged to the child, meaning that £8,105 will be tax-free.

The snag: if the money came from the parents, the £100 limit will apply. The answer: get the grandparent or another relative to set up a bare trust and put the money into an offshore bond. Suppose they put in £50,000, then the trustees could withdraw £5,000 a year. Out of this, £2,500 will be tax-free - withdrawals up to 5% a year from offshore bonds are not subject to immediate tax. The other £2,500 will fall within the child's personal tax allowance, so that will also be tax-free. (This route is also used to help pay for private school fees)

£200,000 TO BRING UP!

The years go by, and overall you spend around £200,000 on food, education, pocket money etc - according to one investment company - in raising your offspring! They would like to go university, you want them to go, so you look at how to pay for university. Being prudent, you expect that they will owe the top-end £50,000 when they graduate in three years' time. (The National Union of Students reckon that taking a degree in London now costs more, just under £23,000 a year).

You, and your son or daughter, will look into the scholarships and bursaries which are available. There should be more of these since tuition fees have been raised - and they do not have to be repaid. Some will be means-tested.

9% OVER £21,000

Once they get a job, your son or daughter will start to repay their student loan in the April after they graduate. Repayment comes through the tax system, and they pay back 9% of everything they earn above £21,000 of pre-tax salary.

The employer takes it off the payroll - the money is adjusted if they lose their job or have to take a salary cut. Any loan still outstanding after 30 years is wiped out. (This £21,000 threshold will be raised in line with inflation from 2016).

NOW A REAL RATE OF INTEREST

The other big change in the loan set-up is that a real rate of interest is being charged from September 2012. Under the old rules, interest was set at the rate of inflation. This meant that there was no real cost to the student, so that financing the loan effectively came free. Now, students pay interest at inflation +3%

while they are studying. After they graduate, they pay higher rates of interest the more they earn:
Up to £21,000 - inflation;
£21,000-£41,000 - tapered rise up to inflation+3%, and
Over £41,000 - inflation+3%.

Suppose that the new graduate lands one of the higher-paid jobs in law or finance. He should fairly quickly get to £41,000 a year. From then on - assuming today's inflation rate - he will be paying 5-6% interest. By the time the loan is paid off, his interest bill could have doubled the amount he owed. (If he had repaid his loan down to £40,000 by the time he reached that salary level, for that year he would repay £1,800 and face an interest bill of £2,000 plus).

Inflation is the key - over the coming years the rate of price rises will make students' loan interest rate acceptable or turn it into a heavy burden. It all depends on whether the Bank of England can keep inflation at the mandated 2% or whether it is allowed to reach 5% or more. Many people, not just graduates, will be watching.

TAX ON GRADUATES

This is a graduate tax system because what the student repays - or whether they repay at all - depends on how much they earn, not on the amount they borrow. The rate of interest they pay does not depend on the size or duration of the loan but on the salary they receive. If the graduate's salary is much below the national average, they will not have to make any repayments. Some people, on salaries around the average, will continue to repay through a large part of their working lives.

CHOICE FOR HIGH-FLYERS

Parents and students need to understand that we are therefore talking tax for a number of years - 20% income tax+9% payback if their salary is less than £34,370 and tax at 40%+9% payback from £34,371 up to £150,000. A high-flyer graduate, who gets a job where he soon starts to pay higher-rate tax, faces a choice.

To avoid interest piling up, some people urge better-paid graduates to make extra loan repayments. This has to depend on the graduate's situation - whether he needs cash for a house deposit and, above all, whether he reckons he can beat the 5-6% net or whatever rate the student loan will be costing him.

HOW TO HELP

Because this is a graduate tax, you the parent need to reflect on how best to help the student, though the best way has to depend on the family situation and the new graduate's personal plans. Many people's reaction, when their child goes to university, is to raise a lump sum from a remortgage or pension fund - but this may not be the best remedy for the graduate's tax bill. Some parents pay university fees upfront, which is an expensive option.

Nor does raising a lump sum make obvious financial sense. When this was written, the maximum interest of inflation+3% equated to 5-6%. That represents a significant increase on the previous rate, but is still less than a bank would charge the student or graduate for an unsecured overdraft, and a good deal less than they would pay borrowing on a credit card.

MAYBE A LET

One way parents help is by buying or renting their offspring a student let - say a two bedroom unit where the student lets the other unit and can benefit from the rent a room scheme, offering £4,250 a year tax free. Parents need to get familiar with this market (some lenders stay away from student lets) and to focus on leading universities where student accommodation is in short supply.

You could offer a lump sum when they start a job and plan to buy their first house or flat - and will be making a 9% payback on top of their 20% standard rate tax bill. Alternatively, you could parcel out the lump sum over several years to ease the impact of the 20+9% charge.

This new starting-point of £21,000 for loan repayment represents a big increase on the old level of £15,795, so that graduates will now have to repay less each year. But you the loans will be larger (mainly because tuition fees are so much higher) and interest rates have increased. The upshot is that people will spend longer paying off their tuition and maintenance loans.

IT DEPENDS WHERE YOU STUDY

When you consider which university your child will go to, whatever they choose could have a financial impact through the different levels of tuition fees. The set-up described here applies to students studying in England and living in England and to all UK students - except Welsh residents - who choose a university outside the country where they live. (Maintenance and in particular property costs also vary)

Rules are different in Scotland, Wales and Northern Ireland. Scottish students studying in Scotland will not pay any tuition fees, Welsh resident students studying anywhere in the UK and Northern Irish students studying in Northern Ireland will have their fees heavily subsidised. Other students face paying up to the maximum £9,000.

CHOOSE THE BANK

When your offspring first gets to university, they need to choose a bank - and some banks may take the initiative and go to them. The banks see today's students as tomorrow's captains of industry and finance - therefore important prospective customers. First step, if the new student already has a bank account, is to make sure that this is rated as a student account. They will get better terms, possibly twice over if they are an existing customer.(one bank gives a free railcard). The second step (before thinking about freebies) is to focus on what matters - getting an interest-free overdraft. This is an important money-saver throughout the student's course. Avoid the banks which charge and look for the major names who will offer an overdraft up to £2,000 or £3,000 interest-free. You need to be clear whether the offer is for £2,000 or 'up to £2,000' and whether the offer is tiered - so much in the first year, and more in the second and third years. For 2012-13 the best offer was a £3,000 straight interest-free overdraft, well worth having.

STAY INTEREST-FREE

Check also if the bank offers special deals for graduates. Some do not, but they may let the student keep their interest-free overdraft for a year after graduating. Some banks ask students to make a small initial deposit or pay a certain amount into the account during their first year - or to make a few transactions every month.

When you discuss with your student son or daughter the freebies which the banks offer, treat these as useful extras - the important deal is the interest-free overdraft. Freebies typically include free travel insurance, a NUS shopping card, price reductions on some electronic equipment. Nice to have, but not a deal-maker.

One set of figures you should impress on the new student is how much the bank will charge for an arranged overdraft and even more for non-arranged borrowing. One bank popular with students will charge 10% interest if the student has to go over the agreed overdraft limit - but that rate will rocket to 16% for an non-arranged borrowing. A 10% rate means that a loan doubles in seven years; at 16% it doubles in less than five. If you can, avoid!

****

Chapter 12

Help From Credit Cards

Credit cards can be a major help when you plan the years from 45 to retirement. You have established a good credit record, you are familiar with financial products and are prepared to take some trouble in order to make money. Credit cards can be made to work for you, but they carry one health warning - if you slip up on the procedures, you could end up paying money at fierce interest rates to the card companies, and perhaps earning a black mark on your credit history. If you do not pay your credit card bills on time, so that you borrow from the card company, you will pay interest anywhere between 10% a year up to 40%.

Many people, it seems, are not prepared to take even a little trouble to make money. Most of us - six out of ten in a 2012 survey by one of the card companies - pay off all of our card bill in full each month. Everyone who clears their balance should use a card which gives them benefits in return, such as vouchers, discounts or just cashback. Yet people still use cash, debit cards or non-reward cards. In the UK, it is estimated that consumers are ignoring benefits worth a staggering £50-£60 million a week,

GET CASHBACK

Cashback is probably the easiest to understand. When you first get the card, you may be offered a come-on rate for a few months of 4% or 5% on your initial spend, probably with a cap of £100 cashback. After that, you will get a straight 1% or 1.25% on everything you buy, apart from cash deals; you may have to pay a small fee. At the end of a year, you will get your cashback by the amount being deducted from your monthly bill.

All these benefits, including cashback, only make sense if you clear your bill every month. Otherwise, the cost of borrowing from the card company would be far greater than what you gained. You should use your cashback card to its maximum extent - as opposed to other credit or debit cards and in place of cash.

USE DIRECT DEBIT

If you do clear your account - or whenever you settle any debt which is owing to the card company - you should use a direct debit arranged with your bank. Credit card payments are essentially time-sensitive and under a direct debit it is the bank's responsibility to pay on time. The alternatives, such as you handing over cash or sending a cheque, can suffer from glitches in the company's handling system or in Royal Mail's operations. You will then pay for being late and perhaps get a black mark on your credit record.

TYPES OF PLASTIC

Maybe some people miss out on benefits because they are confused by plastic. These are the principal types:

Credit Card: you make your purchase, you get a bill anything up to two months later and after a few weeks you pay the card company.

Store Card: credit card run by retailers such as John Lewis and Marks & Spencer, you get a reward in vouchers which you can use in-store.

Charge Card: same procedure as a credit card, but you settle your bill in full each month - no credit element.

Debit Card: moves money from your bank account, rather like a plastic cheque - no credit element.

Prepaid/Loaded Card: you first put money onto the card, and then handle it like any other card; loaded cards are often used to draw cash from ATMs in the UK and abroad as well as for spending - no credit element.

Until the last few years, credit cards usually came free. Now, a number of card companies are charging fees - around £25 'to cover administration' or larger amounts to pay for services they provide - travel insurance, car breakdown, maybe a concierge function to book restaurants or holidays. This is like the banks' offering services with their premier accounts, and you should look at them in the same way:

(a)which of the services do you want and will you use, and

(b)could you buy them separately for less?

SHOP AT 0%

Cashback attracts many people, but you are simply getting back a very small proportion of what you have already spent. Many people want credit to help their financial plan - which points to interest-free shopping followed by a balance transfer.

Interest-free shopping means that you can use your card, for nine to 12 months, with no interest to pay on what you buy. You are being given an interest-free loan, equal to the amount of your credit limit. You will have to make a minimum repayment each month, though that may be a little as 1-2% of your bill. You must always stay within the debt ceiling which the card company arranged when you took out the card.

NEW CUSTOMERS PREFERRED

One caution: the card companies aim interest-free shopping primarily at new customers. This means that you will probably not be able to get a 0% shopping card if it is one which you already own or which you have held some time over the past year or so.

At the end of the nine to 12 months, you have a choice. You may be able to repay what you owe. Alternatively, you could do nothing, which means that your interest bill would climb from zero to the card company's usual lending rate. Or you could, like most people faced by this hike in interest cost, go for a balance transfer.

TRANSFER A BALANCE

A balance transfer means just what it says - you transfer your debt from credit card X to credit card Y. Your new card company is keen to attract customers, so it offers you 0% interest on the amount you transfer for anything from nine months up to two years. The new balance will involve a one-off fee, typically 2-3% but it is worth checking around. Some card companies will offer reduced fees for a limited period.

You can transfer other credit or store card balances - but you should aim not to have outstanding debt on your store cards.

These are sold in-store, often with the appeal of a price reduction on the goods you are buying. You will find that most store cards charge higher interest rates than credit cards. So take the retailer's price reduction, and any similar benefits to come in the future - but try to avoid borrowing.

SIMPLE TO MOVE

Using a balance transfer you can move outstanding debts from different cards and handily put what you owe in one place. Procedures are simple - you just have to decide from which cards you want to move the balances, and how much. At the end of the period, the interest rate will go up sharply from zero to the card company's usual rate.

All this looks highly cost-effective: you have had a year's shopping at 0% interest, then a further year or more with a balance transfer giving credit also at 0% interest. Your only cost over the entire two to three years has been the 2-3% fee, when you arranged the balance transfer. So why not keep repeating the process?

NEW SERIES NEEDED

That looks appealing, but to make it work you would need a whole series of new credit cards offering what you want - which many people's finances would not support. Your debt ceiling would be raised with each new card, and some companies set relatively high debt levels hoping to attract business.

Card holders' reaction is often to ask for lower debt limits, but this needs to be handled with care. One of the basic credit tests, which a new lender or card company are likely to use, is to compare the amount of credit you need with the total you have agreed with all the various card companies. If you reduce your limit on a card, you will be using a bigger proportion of the amount of credit you have available - which is usually a negative indicator on someone's credit record.

CARD COMPANY ON THE HOOK

Most people now appreciate that they should use a credit card when they make a sizeable purchase - especially an appliance or furniture. If there is a problem, or the supplier goes bust, the law decrees that you can look to the credit card company.

Under the law, both the credit card company and the seller are responsible, in the UK and overseas, for any misrepresentation or fault in the original contract. The law also lays down that the transaction must be between £100 and £30,000. But if your deal falls outside these limits, it is still worth contacting the bank which issued your card.

'Credit' is the key word for this protection. If there is no credit element in the deal, you will not be covered in this way. So a credit card will work for you, but a charge card or a debit card will not.

YOU PAY TO CHANGE

Using your card abroad needs further reflection (see the chapter on holiday money). Most cards charge a commission to translate your dollar or euro bill into pounds - generally around 3%. A few do not, and these are the ones you should take on holiday -

Halifax, Nationwide, Post Office, Saga. Remember also to use these commission-free cards when you buy over the net something which is priced in dollars or euros.

With credit cards and charge cards, you are getting credit from the card company. But you can reverse the process - load money onto your card before you use it. Using a loaded or prepaid card is the best way to get currency from an ATM when you go abroad - and you can use a prepaid card back home if you want to budget or give cash to a teenager going off to university.

LESS TO LOSE

Loaded cards are easy to get: there is no credit, so no credit check.(but therefore no consumer credit protection)If a villain takes your loaded card, the maximum at risk is the amount you have loaded - he cannot work his way from the card into your bank account.

Plastic makes life simpler for everybody(around 70 million cards held in the UK) - which the villains also understand. If you lose your card, contact the card company at once. But you could lose while it sits in your wallet. All the thief needs is the number, code, expiry date(maybe copied by a crooked waiter in a restaurant) and your billing address. He can then spend over the net and you will never know - until some puzzling bills arrive.

So you look after your card as if it were cash. You have a legal obligation to take 'reasonable care' of your credit card - which means, among other things, not letting it out of your sight. Do not leave your card if you are running a tab at a bar, when the bill may turn out to be far larger than you expected (especially likely when you are celebrating abroad). If that happens, you are not likely to get any sympathy, or compensation, from the card company or the ombudsman.

Follow these basic rules:

- Go through every monthly statement you get from the card company. If there is something you do not recognise, contact them by phone and confirm in writing. Do not throw the statements away - shred them when you are finished.
- Every six months, check over your credit file, which you can buy for a few pounds from one of the credit agencies. Correct any mistakes, which you are entitled to do.
- Take care with passwords and customer numbers. You may be asked for your mother's maiden name and your birth date as part of a security check. Both of these are on public record, so if you are asked, make them up.
- Never quote your card number or any sensitive data in e-mails - they are not secure. On the net, buy only from a secure site.

****

Chapter 13

Think Outside the Box

You are now 45, pondering your financial planning for retirement, and you occasionally fee just a little downhearted. Shares are worth less than they were 10 years ago. Interest rates on savings are low - barely covering tax and inflation. When you decide to retire and buy a pension, you find that the Bank of England's 'quantitative easing' has pushed annuity rates down to their lowest level for years.

So you sometimes feel that the conventional methods have not worked too well. Why not think outside the box, at least for part of your assets - 10% or maybe even 20%? You have to accept that when you step outside the box, you may step away from the Financial Services Authority - which means that you will not be covered by the Financial Services Compensation Scheme if things go wrong. You feel you can face that - you are only thinking about a part of your assets. Your first thoughts turn to wine. You and your friends enjoy drinking wine - what about an investment?

GROWTH IN WINE

The investment figures look appealing - 15% a year average growth over the recent past, though with some ups and downs. You do not need to have extensive knowledge of wine, but you do need to choose an established wine merchant. As the first step, you decide how much you want to invest.

The merchant then buys the wine, insures it and puts it in a temperature-controlled bonded warehouse, so no duty is payable. You wait for a few years (two to five are probably the minimum) and then you sell through the wine merchant or a related broking exchange.

You can invest a few hundred pounds, but a wine merchant who handles investment will probably advise you to think of a minimum £10,000. This could make it a good idea to form an investment syndicate with some like-minded friends.

MAYBE A WASTING ASSET?

The tax position is relatively easy - any 'wasting asset' with a predictable life up to 50 years is free from gains tax. Some fine wines and port have longer lives, but then you can benefit from the 'chattels' exemption. This will keep you out of gains tax when you sell for less than £6,000 and there is tapering relief above that.

The principal tax risk that the HMRC treats you as a wine dealer rather than a collector, so that your profits become taxable. The law is less than perfectly clear on what distinguishes a dealer from a collector.

PERHAPS PHILATELY?

Being a collector means, to many people, being a stamp collector, i.e. a philatelist. An index of rare stamps has outperformed the stock market though a large part of the last 20 years, though with a major hiccup after the 1970s. You can build your own collection, which is a specialist occupation, and where you will be advised to buy stamps only from the 19th century - nothing from the last 60 years.

The alternative is to go to a dealer who will put together a portfolio for you. He probably will not charge when you invest but will take a slice of the profits when you cash in. (Russian, Chinese and Indian stamps have been in demand as local investors start to buy). Expect to pay capital gains tax on your profits.

OR THINK TREES

Some people looking outside the box regard wine and stamps as less than serious, and prefer farmland and forestry. These also offer tax advantages in the UK, but the investment size tends to be relatively large. There are a few timber funds which offer longer-term prospects of defence against inflation. The investment appeal is that timber prices do not move in line with shares and funds can invest in timber via a range of countries and currencies. Timber suppliers can control how much product they put on the market, though prices can be affected say by the amount of new house building in the US.

BEAT THE MARKET

Wine, stamps and trees have their appeal but you decide, after all, that you want to exploit the market you know - the stock exchange. But this time you plan to approach the market in a different way.

Everyone knows that the key to stock market investing is to buy cheap and sell dear. One system, known as momentum investing, is claimed by its supporters to do just that. To make it work you use the net to log three lines on a chart -

- the share index on a weekly basis;
- the average of the index over the previous 30 weeks, and
- the average over the previous 50 weeks.

When the 30-week line goes above the 50-week line, you buy. When the 30-week line falls below the 50-week line, you sell. The aim is to put you into the stock market when it starts to rise and to take you out when it begins to fall.

The system's supporters claim that momentum investing will get most decisions right. It will not anticipate a sudden change, such as the collapse of Northern Rock (no system will). Momentum investing will probably work best when it can identify clear trends in the stock market - less well (as in 2011-12) when the stock market is volatile, without any clear direction.

TWO WAYS TO OUT-PERFORM

Many people have enjoyed a happy retirement because they were clever or lucky enough to beat the market. If you believe you can out-perform the average, there are two principal ways you can do it - contracts for difference or spread betting. Contracts for Difference (CFDs) allow you to make money from share price changes without having to buy the shares. You go to a broker and decide whether the share price will go up or down. You go 'long' if you think the price will rise and you go 'short' if you want to gamble on the price falling. CFDs became popular post-crunch, enabling private investors to go short of shares which they thought were going to be vulnerable.

CASH ON CONTRACT

On a CFD you will pay between 10% and 25% of the share's actual value (there is no stamp duty because you never own the shares). The key to a CFD deal is that cash changes hands when the contract closes - the broker pays you if you called correctly, or you pay him if you get it wrong. You will pay gains tax on your profits.

CFDs are risky, because you could lose more money than you put down to start with. When a share price moves the opposite way to what you expected, you face a tough decision. Do you close the contract and cut your losses - or do you let the contract run, hoping that the share price will move your way?

OR SPREAD BETTING

If you want to gamble on a price movement - in a share, a commodity or the stock market as a whole - you might look at spread betting. This is gambling, less flexible than a CFD but no stamp duty and no tax to pay on the profits you make.

The spread is the dealing spread, the buy/sell difference which the broker will quote to you (the narrower the spread, the better for the customer). Here is how it works:

- the broker quotes 100 (to sell)-102(to buy) share X for the agreed period - a spread of 2;
- you believe that share X will go up, so you buy at 102;
- you stake £5 a point, so you get £5 for every point that share X goes above 102;
- the price closes at 110, so you gain 8x£5=£40.

If the price had closed at 94, you would have lost 8x£5=£40. If you had foreseen the price fall, you would have 'shorted' share X by buying the sell option at 100. When the price fell to 94, you would have won 6x£5=£30.

Anyone who uses spread betting at all frequently should set up a stop-loss limit. Your position will then be closed automatically when you reach the maximum amount that you are prepared to lose.

****

Chapter 14

Keep It Safe

You have built up your assets for retirement, you have put your affairs into good financial order. But you realise that there are people out there who would like to separate you from what you own.

This strikes you when you first appreciate how much about you is known to the public. People can access your birth certificate and your marriage certificate, so they know your full name, your date of birth and your mother's maiden name. You bought shares, so you go on the company's share register which is open to everyone. This gives your name and address and may show that you own a large shareholding - so you look like someone with money, liable to arouse a villain's interest.

DATA ON THE REGISTER

You probably did not think very hard about the electoral register. By law, you have to provide information which generally includes your name, address, nationality and age. All this will appear in the full register, which is published every year and which you will probably find in your public library. You have the chance to opt out of the edited register, which contains the same information and can be sold to anyone who wants to buy it.

Why bother, many people feel. Here is one reason - in summer 2012, villains used someone's name, address and age to raise payday loans in that person's identity, and diverting the proceeds to their own account. The innocent person should avoid any financial loss - the payday lender will suffer - but he will have hassle and might get an undeserved black mark on his credit record.

WALLET TEST

For most people, security centres on credit cards(see the earlier chapter)where the key message is - never let your cards out of your sight, and always check your monthly statements. A security professional will also tell you of the wallet test: you should know exactly what it contains, you should have copies of any cards and if you carry PIN details these should be disguised, say as telephone numbers.(revealing your PIN could cost you compensation). Be alert to the familiar warning signs of a villain's interest. Such as when you order a new cheque book from the bank, but it does not arrive. When you move house, some letters could fall into the wrong hands.

People may phone you out of the blue trying to sell you shares (which may not exist) or plots of land which will shoot up in value if they get planning permission.(which is not going to happen). If the callers are a little more subtle, they will offer you research or analysis, which is meant to lead to you buying from them.

KEEP SAYING NO

You just have to stay polite but very firm, keep saying No, tell the Financial Services Authority and register your telephone number with a call prevention agency.

You will probably have been contacted by a 'boiler room' which is based outside the UK, made up of people who are making 250 calls a day trying to sell something to good persons like yourself.

There are some familiar tricks - if the villains are using a bogus bank, its name will be similar to a genuine high street bank. The villains may look into your background and try 'affinity fraud' when they target a particular group of people.

Many present-day share scams - maybe presented in the topical disguise of investments in solar power or eco-friendly fuel - are a variant on some very old frauds. The 'Spanish prisoner' fraud is said to be several hundred years old: the prisoner needs cash to pay a fine, bribe the warder or whatever. When he gets free, he can access a large sum of money which he will share with you. The come-on is that your modest cash spend will turn into serious money - none of which will ever happen.

FSA=FSCS

Villains contact you in order to get their hands on what you own, but you may lose money as a result of your own financial decisions. Some people make profits from investing in wine or buying stamps (see the previous chapter) but they have stepped away from the Financial Services Authority and, as a result, from the Financial Services Compensation Scheme.

One notable case in recent years was a company which took monthly payments enabling people to buy a hamper at Xmas. The company collapsed, its business was outside the remit of the FSA and therefore the FSCS, so all the contributors could do was go to court - generally an expensive, risky and time-consuming option.

Most people appreciate that there is no safety net when you make up your own mind and buy shares or unit trusts. You may use an adviser on share buying, probably more likely over a pension or insurance issue. You will check that the adviser is registered with the FSA. With an adviser, you have someone to turn to.

KNOW THE RULES

Even when all goes well, it makes sense to know the rules to follow if a problem arises and you have to complain. To make your complaint you have to start with the adviser and take a minimum eight weeks, then go ahead if you are still unhappy with his final response - or if he just ignores you. You contact the ombudsman service, or go to court.

The key to you getting compensation is that the adviser was at fault. Your investment may have collapsed, but that of itself is not enough. You have to be able to show that the adviser was negligent - say by putting you into investments which were outside the risk areas you had agreed with him.

A MADOFF?

Most people take care over their financial planning and do not bother too much about security - until they hit a Madoff. For serious investors, a Madoff is the biggest single worry. Madoff built up a large fund in the US and the UK, which showed good performance and attracted numbers of sophisticated investors across the world. And it was a fake.

For years, Madoff ran a huge Ponzi scheme (see the glossary)where dividends were paid out of money contributed by new investors - not from underlying profits. When the world-wide crunch arrived after 2007, new investment dried up and the Madoff structure fell apart. Lawyers and accountants have been working since then to recover money for investors.

WAYS TO SPOT

How do you, a serious but layman investor, spot a Madoff? You read the literature you get from fund managers and you become suspicious if performance stays good and you do not understand why - you always need to know the reasons for good or bad news. Remember the fraud squad's advice: 'if it looks too good to be true, it probably is.'

You read the back pages of the manager's brochures(it is often a good idea to read from the back)where you check that the trustee is solid and - especially - that the auditor is one of the leading international firms. You read press comments on the managers and on your own fund and you check out the directors, using your favourite search engine.

DIVERSIFY

All these sensible   actions might have kept you away from Madoff, but there is only one sure way - diversify. 'Do not put all your eggs in one basket' has to be one of the fundamentals in financial safety. It cuts across what could be the chance of a lifetime, when you see the next Apple or Amazon and want to buy the shares and invest all the money you can lay your hands on.

If that happens, you are looking at risk - how much risk you accept depends on you, your situation and your commitments. This is one thing you, and only you, can decide.

****

GLOSSARY - WHAT FINANCIAL TERMS MEAN

Absolute Return Fund: a fund which aims to make a positive return whether the stock market rises or falls. Some funds charge a performance fee. (see Hedge Funds)

Basis Points: how the markets describe interest rates, where 100 basis points equal 1%.

Beta Factor: measures the riskiness of a share by comparing its price movements with those of the market as a whole.

BRIC: term coined to refer to the four major emerging-market economies - Brazil, Russia, India, China.

CPI: consumer prices index, now used by the government rather than RPI, the retail prices index. CPI excludes housing costs.(see RPI)

Carry Trade: borrow in a currency where interest rates are low (often Japan)to lend in a currency where rates are high(typically Europe) Currency fluctuations can make this risky.

Chapter 11: Bankruptcy protection in the US. A company's obligations to its creditors are postponed, giving it time to reorganise.

Collateralised Debt Obligation(CDO): a financial structure which groups bonds and other debt into a portfolio which can then be traded. In theory, the spread of risk should improve the credit rating.

Credit Default Swap: a type of financial insurance. The buyer of the swap pays the seller in return for protection if a loan defaults.

Credit Rating Agency: companies such as Standard & Poor, Moody's, Fitch, which publish ratings on debt issued by companies and countries. Changes in the ratings of countries' loans reflect Eurozone debt issues.

Current/Running Yield: the current level of income expressed as a percentage of the bond or share price.

Default: when a company, or a country, fails to meet the interest or repayment obligations which are due on its debt. Default may have to be decided by courts or a tribunal - as happened to Greece.

Deleveraging: reducing the level of borrowings - as the government and individuals in the UK aim to do.

Derivatives: assets whose value is fixed by reference to(so derived from)other assets. Options to buy shares represent a basic derivative.

Double Dip: when an economy, which had been in recession, recovers but then slips back (as it would appear when drawn on a chart).

Equity Release: a way to realise the value of your house(equity=current value minus debt)often by a lifetime mortgage, where interest is rolled up.

Eurobor: Interest rate at which banks in Europe lend to one another.(see Libor)

Futures: a futures contract is an agreement to buy or sell currency or a commodity at a pre-arranged date and price. Can be used to hedge or speculate.

GDP: gross domestic product. Measures the economic activity in a country.

Gross Redemption Yield: the yield, generally on a bond, which takes into account the gain or loss over the buying price if the bond is held to maturity.

Hedge Funds: these aim to make money whatever the stock market conditions, e.g. by investing in commodities as well as shares and by using financial assets such as derivatives.(see also Absolute Return funds)

IMA: the UK Investment Management Association, which categorises the investment management industry into more than 30 sectors.

Identity Theft: when a criminal finds out your personal details and uses these to buy goods and get credit cards and a passport.

Impaired Life Annuities: annuities offering a better rate than average to people who smoke, work in strenuous occupations or have a history of illness.

IPO: Initial Public Offering, when a privately owned business goes public. (Wall Street terminology)

Junk Bond: a bond which carries a high rate of interest to compensate the buyer for a high risk of default. Junk is the lowest credit rating, currently applied to Greece.

KIID: Key Investor Information Document. EU rules require unit trust buyers to confirm they have read the relevant KIID.

LIBOR: London Inter Bank Offered Rate. The rate at which banks lend money to one another. A major issue in 2012 when some banks were accused of rigging the rate.

Lifestyle Option: when an insurance company or an adviser moves investments from shares into cash and bonds as the holder approaches retirement - or he does it himself.

Loaded card: a prepaid card, which can be used in the UK or abroad for spending and at ATMs.

Mark to Market: when banks and others have to show assets at market values, as opposed to their own valuations, sometimes on a monthly or even daily basis. When markets fall, this can cause capital adequacy problems.

Monetary Policy Committee: the Bank of England group which meets weekly to fix the level of Bank Rate.

Money Laundering: moving money made from crime into the mainstream financial system.

Option: an agreement which gives the right, but not the obligation, to buy or sell an asset at a pre-agreed price at a pre-agreed time. You can walk away from an option, by simply letting it lapse.

PIGS: countries in the Eurozone with national debt problems - Portugal, Ireland, Greece, Spain. A current question is whether Italy should be included.

Payday lenders: financial companies which lend unsecured short-term money, often over the net at a few hours' notice, and charge high rates of interest.

Ponzi scheme: a scam where dividends are paid not out of profits but from the capital invested by new shareholders. Bernie Madoff ran the biggest-ever Ponzi scheme. (Charles Ponzi was a US operator in the 1920s)Also known as pyramid selling.

Quantitative Easing(QE): when the Bank of England puts credit into the banking system by buying assets such as government bonds. Major risk is that QE will push up inflation.

Quartile Ranking: used to measure how well a fund performed against its competitors. Top 25% are the first quartile, the next 25% second quartile, and so on.

Recession: when incomes or output decline for two successive quarters.

Redemption yield: return on a bond or gilt-edged which allows for the capital profit or loss when it matures.

Retail Price Index(RPI): the traditional measure of price inflation for consumers(see CPI)

Securitisation: when a variety of debts(mortgages, credit card debt, student loans)are packaged together in a company whose shares can be traded.

Short selling: when an investor borrows shares to sell, aiming to buy them back more cheaply when they fall - and so make his profit.(in a 'naked short' the investor does not borrow)

Stagflation: the combination of low growth and price inflation - as in the UK in 2011-12.

Structured Investment: a fund where the return is based on the performance of a pre-determined share index.

Sub Prime: housing loans made to borrowers with a poor financial history.(the borrowers are called ninjas - no income, no job, no assets)

Tier 1 Capital: test of a bank's strength, through the amount of its shares, disclosed reserves and retained profits.

Total Expense Ratio: the total cost of running a fund - annual charge by the manager, plus legal, custody and accounting costs.

Toxic Debt: loans made by banks which are unlikely to be repaid in full - or maybe not repaid at all. Toxic debts can be hived off into 'bad banks.'(in the US, toxic debt is sometimes called 'legacy assets')

Trail commission: annual commission which a unit trust manager pays to a broker so long as his client continues to hold the manager's units.

Underlying yield: generally applied to a bond unit trust, to show annualised income after deducting the Total Expense Ratio.

Warrant: a document giving the right to buy a share at a stated price at a stated time - similar to an option, but warrants are often listed separately on the stock market.

Write-Down: reducing the balance sheet value of an asset to bring it into line with the market or to reflect a changed situation.

Yield Gap: the difference in yield between shares and bonds - often regarded as a guide to stock market prospects.

Useful addresses and websites

Association of Investment
Trust Companies (AITC)
Durrant House
8-13 Chiswell Street
London EC1Y 4YY
Hotline: 020 7282 5555
www.aitc.co.uk

Debt Management Office
Eastcheap Court
11 Philpot Lane
London EC3M 8UD
Tel: 0845 357 6500
www.dmo.gov.uk

Department for Work and Pensions (DWP)
If you ring The Pension Service on 0845 606 0265,
You will be connected to the pension centre covering you area,
Or you can look on the website (www.
thepensionservice.gov.uk/contact)

You can obtain DWP leaflets from Pension Service and
Jobcentre Plus office and some post offices, CABs or
Libraries. You can write to:

Pension Guides
Freepost
Bristol BS38 7WA
Tel: 08457 31 32 33
If you have access to the Internet, you can download the leaflets
(and claim forms for many of the benefits)
from www.dwp.gov. uk or www.thepensionservice.gov.uk

Financial Ombudsman
Service (FOS)

South Quay Plaza
183 Marsh Wall
London E14 9SR
Consumer helpline: 0845 080 1800
www.financialombudsman.org,uk

Financial Services Authority (FSA)
25 The North Colonnade
Canary Wharf
London E14 5HS
Consumer helpline: 0845 606 1234
www.fsa.gov.uk/consumer

HM Revenue & Customs (HMRC)
The government department that deals
With al;most all the taxes due in the UK.
Most HMRC leaflets can be obtained
From local tax offices or Tax Enquiry Centres
(look for in the phone book under `Revenue'
or `Government Department') or Jobcentre Plus offices.
Almost all are also available on the website at:
www.hmrc.gov.uk or you can ring them the Orderline:
Tel: 0845 900 0404

HM Revenue & Customs National Insurance
Contributions Office (NICO)
Benton Park View
Newcastle upon Tyne NE98 1ZZ
Enquiry Line: 0845 302 1479

International Pension Centre
The Pension Service
Tyneview Park
Newcastle upon Tyne NE98 1BA
Tel: 01912 187777
(8.00am-8.00pm,weekdays)

Investment Management Association
65 Kingsway
London WC2B 6TD
Tel: 020 7831 0898
Information line 020 7269 4639
www.investmentfunds.org.uk
(OEIC.S).

The Pension Service
State Pension Forecasting Team
Future Pension Centre
Tyneview Park
Whitley Road Newcastle upon Tyne NE98 1BA
Tel: 0845 3000 168
www.thepensionservice.gove.uk

Pension Tracing Service
Tel: 0845 600 2537
www.thepensionservice.gov.uk

Pension Advisory Service
(TPAS)
11 Belgrave Road
London SW1V 1RB
Helpline: 0845 601 2923
www.pensionsadvisoryservice.org.uk

Specialist Magazines
Money Management
3rd Floor
Maple House
149 Tottenham Court Road
London W1P 9LL
020 8606 7545

Planned Savings
6-77 Paul Street

London EC2A 4LG
020 753 1000
Money management and Planned Savings are aimed at
professional advisers.

Trade Bodies

The Association of Investment Trust Companies
9th Floor
24 Chiswell Street
London EC1Y 4YY
0207 282 5555
www.itsonline.co.uk www.aitc.co.uk

Provides information on aspects of investing in investment trust
companies.

The Investment Management Association
65 Kingsway
London WC2B 6TD
020 7269 4639
 www.investmentuk.org
Provides information on investing in unit trusts and Oeics

Proshare
4th Floor Bankside House
107 Leadenhall Street
London EC3A 4AF
0906 802 2222
www.proshare.org.uk

Advises on setting up investment clubs and runs education
programmes for schools on share ownership

The Association of British Insurers
51 Gresham Street
London EC2V 7HQ

020 7600 333
www.abi.org.uk
Publishes information sheets on all aspects of insurance.

The British Insurance Brokers Association
14 Bevis Marks
London EC3A 7NT
0901 814 0015
www.biba.org.uk
www.bsa.org.uk

Borrowing

The National Debtline
0808 808 4000
 The Association of British Credit Unions
Holyoake House
Hanover Street
Manchester M60 OAS
0161 832 8694
www.abcul.org

Credit Information Agencies
Experian
Consumer help services
PO Box 8000
Nottingham NG1 5GX
0870 241 6212
www.experian.com

Equifax Europe (UK)
Credit file advice centre
PO Box 3001
Glasgow G81 0583
0870 010 0583
www.equifax.co.uk

Investment information websites

www.investment-gateway.com
www.new-online-investor.co.uk
www.find.co.uk

Index

www.straightforwardco.co.uk

All titles, listed below, in the Straightforward Guides Series can be purchased online, using credit card or other forms of payment by going to www.straightfowardco.co.uk A discount of 25% per title is offered with online purchases.

Law
A Straightforward Guide to:
Consumer Rights
Bankruptcy Insolvency and the Law
Employment Law
Private Tenants Rights
Family law
Small Claims in the County Court
Contract law
Intellectual Property and the law
Divorce and the law
Leaseholders Rights
The Process of Conveyancing
Knowing Your Rights and Using the Courts
Producing Your own Will
Housing Rights
The Bailiff the law and You
Probate and The Law
Company law
What to Expect When You Go to Court
Guide to Competition Law
Give me Your Money-Guide to Effective Debt Collection
Caring for a Disabled Child

General titles
Letting Property for Profit
Buying, Selling and Renting property
Buying a Home in England and France
Bookkeeping and Accounts for Small Business
Creative Writing
Freelance Writing

Writing Your own Life Story
Writing performance Poetry
Writing Romantic Fiction
Speech Writing
Teaching Your Child to Read and write
Teaching Your Child to Swim
Raising a Child-The Early Years
Creating a Successful Commercial Website
The Straightforward Business Plan
The Straightforward C.V.
Successful Public Speaking
Handling Bereavement
Play the Game-A Compendium of Rules
Individual and Personal Finance
Understanding Mental Illness
The Two Minute Message
Guide to Self Defence
Buying a Used Car
Tiling for Beginners

Go to:

www.straightforwardco.co.uk